A〈
Dry B

M000301192

"Brandan Robertson is one of the most astute young Christian writers. His compelling new book, deeply rooted in the Bible, shows how Scripture can inform the most contemporary of questions, and help us lead the most spiritual of lives."

— James Martin, SJ
author, *Jesus: A Pilgrimage* and Learning to Pray

"When the future feels perilous, people of faith often turn to the past for guidance and hope. Our Christian traditions and ancient scriptures can function like anchors, fixing us firmly in place when the winds of social change threaten to blow us into the dark waters of disillusionment. In *Dry Bones and Holy Wars*, Brandan Robertson offers readers deft theological reflections on the biggest sources of our current cultural angst—social polarization, political corruption, spiritual abuse, ecological disaster—leveraging the wisdom of the Christian tradition to fuel subversive hope. Robertson's writing blends a pastor's heart and an activist's instincts, and the result is a book of haunting provocation that refuses to be ignored."

— Jonathan Merritt
contributing writer, *The Atlantic*
author, *Learning to Speak God from Scratch*

"In an age of political divisions, intense polarization, climate crisis, and war, Robertson offers a series of reflections that look back at biblical narratives to help us face our present with wisdom, humility, and kindness so we can create together a future of hope, justice, and right relationships. He reminds us that God is still with us, inviting us into life-giving faith."

— Bishop Karen Oliveto
The Mountain Sky Conference of The United Methodist Church

"In this moment of unprecedented cultural upheaval and social challenge, people of faith have looked to their traditions to find guidance and hope. In *Dry Bones and Holy Wars*, Brandan Robertson offers a challenging biblical call for followers of Jesus to embrace the prophetic nature of our tradition and lean into this moment with radical compassion and subversive hope for creating a more just and equal world."

— Rev. Dr. Jacqueline Lewis
senior minister, Middle Church; author, *Fierce Love*

"The sea has parted, and a massive exodus of disaffected evangelical Christians is pouring into the desert. Exiles suffering from spiritual thirst should seek out Brandan Robertson, who has taken the trek himself. This book shows the way to the oasis of a much kinder, gentler Christianity."

—Jim Burklo
senior associate dean of religious and spiritual life
University of Southern California
author, *Tenderly Calling: An Invitation to the Way of Jesus*

"*Dry Bones and Holy Wars* demonstrates the timeless beauty and power of the Word for each generation. As Millennials and Gen Z are turning away from the church and the Bible, Robertson's message invites them to consider again the wisdom of the Bible stories interpreted with new eyes and heard with new ears and all coming from the same eternal source of love."

—Rev. Rich Tafel
pastor, Church of the Holy City, Washington, D.C.

"Never before has humanity faced such a wide range of strategic, geopolitical, environmental and societal challenges. How do we respond to the fears, insecurities and uncertainties of our turbulent world? Brandan Robertson offers us a compelling vision of a more just, inclusive and equitable future—radical new thinking soaked in ancient biblical wisdom, compassion and hope."

—Rev. Steve Chalke
founder, Oasis Global

Dry Bones and Holy Wars

Dry Bones and Holy Wars

A Call for Social and
Spiritual Renewal

Brandan Robertson

ORBIS BOOKS
www.orbisbooks.com

ORBIS BOOKS
www.orbisbooks.com

Fathers and Brothers
MARYKNOLL

Founded in 1970, Orbis Books endeavors to publish works that enlighten the mind, nourish the spirit, and challenge the conscience. The publishing arm of the Maryknoll Fathers and Brothers, Orbis seeks to explore the global dimensions of the Christian faith and mission, to invite dialogue with diverse cultures and religious traditions, and to serve the cause of reconciliation and peace. The books published reflect the views of their authors and do not represent the official position of the Maryknoll Society. To learn more about Maryknoll and Orbis Books, please visit our website at www.orbisbooks.com

Manufactured in the United States of America

Library of Congress Cataloging-in-Publication Data

Names: Robertson, Brandan, 1992– author.
Title: Dry bones and holy wars : a call for social and spiritual renewal / Brandon Robertson.
Description: Maryknoll, New York : Orbis Books, [2022] | Includes bibliographical references. | Summary: "Reflections rooted in the biblical tradition, tied to pressing modern concerns, inviting Christians and others to individual and communal introspection"— Provided by publisher.
Identifiers: LCCN 2022007665 (print) | LCCN 2022007666 (ebook) | ISBN 9781626984974 (trade paperback) | ISBN 9781608339594 (epub)
Subjects: LCSH: Church renewal. | Christianity and culture.
Classification: LCC BV600.3 .R623 2022 (print) | LCC BV600.3 (ebook) | DDC 262.001/7—dc23/eng/20220601
LC record available at https://lccn.loc.gov/2022007665
LC ebook record available at https://lccn.loc.gov/2022007666

To Cheryl Starbuck, whose love, encouragement, and support helped me through the turbulent years that this book was written and continues to energize and inspire me today. *Thank you.*

Contents

Preface

When I entered seminary in 2015, it was clear that there were seismic shifts happening in our world, shifts that would inevitably require clergy of all traditions to lean deeper into our calling to be both prophets and healers throughout the coming decades. Polarization was on the rise and existential threats like climate change were becoming more dire. From where I sat as a young, wide-eyed optimist with quite a bit of privilege, I felt like we were making progress as a nation and as a species. But by the time I graduated in 2017, my perspective shifted dramatically.

The US presidential campaigns of 2016–17 began to unearth a startling reality for many citizens—that despite the superficial progress we seemed to have made, much of the deep-seated prejudice, hatred, and apathy toward injustice that we often spoke of as a bygone era had been flourishing just beneath the surface of our nation's collective consciousness. White supremacy, antisemitism, misogyny, homophobia, transphobia, nationalism—all of this reared its ugly head not just in the speeches of Donald Trump but in the millions of people who supported him, including a stunning number of Christian religious leaders.

As I contemplated what it meant for me to step into the role of a Christian pastor in this era, I admit that I was quite timid. I knew that wherever I ended up, I would need to draw on my faith tradition to speak hard truths about our collective sins and our need for repentance and transformation. I knew that throughout the Trump presidency, I would be challenged to encourage Christian resistance to the often-backward ethics and xenophobic policies of the Trump administration, which would likely result in a lot of pushback from those who wanted to keep their faith and politics separate. In short, as I accepted my first call, I knew that the first few years of my ministry would be challenging to say the least.

I had no clue just how challenging they would turn out to be. Nearly every month from 2017 to 2020, there was some major tragedy or moment of reckoning. From the murder of George Floyd to a global pandemic to the January 6 insurrection, my role as a pastor began to look more like that of a community organizer. I would spend large portions of my days working with local coalitions to mobilize my congregation to participate in tangible action to demand justice and bring healing to the world. Our Sunday worship services began to seem like organizing meetings, with my sermon being a moment where I would remind the congregation of our moral responsibility as disciples of Jesus and then point to individual and collective actions we could all take to transform the brokenness around us through subversive acts of truth telling and love. My counseling sessions were often focused on helping people process their bewilderment and fear about the state of the world. And I found myself spending a lot of time wrestling with my own perspective and beliefs through writing.

What you are holding is a series of reflections I have written to help myself and fellow Christians process the moment we are living in and how we should respond to it. Each reflection is rooted in the ancient biblical tradition and tied to a pressing modern concern, inviting us to individual and communal introspection about how we have arrived here and how we can move forward as a people. While the events that provoked these reflections are now past, we are still living in the ongoing impact of these realities, and, thus, continued faithful reflection and response is merited.

These words are offered not as answers to our society's many ills but as provocations to new ways of seeing and being in the world. It is my hope that these words will serve to inspire innovative ways of thinking about how modern disciples of Jesus might embody our faith in the world and ultimately bring you some encouragement and hope that a more just world is not only possible but is well within our reach.

1

Tear Down Those Walls

In moments of social unrest, we often look to religion to help give us guidance and hope. Our faith is supposed to help us navigate moments of upheaval and turmoil in our lives; yet many of us have discovered that when we turn to our faith, or even more specifically, our faith communities, we find that the divisions and turmoil are just as real and are often even intensified within the institution of faith. I have often found myself wondering why I even continue to be a part of religion when more and more frequently it seems that religious people are exacerbating the social issues we're collectively facing.

But in the midst of this cynicism, I turn to the pages of Scripture and continue to find profound wisdom and guidance. Sure, there is much to critique about the Bible, yet this collection of writings has endured for thousands of years because within it is a deep understanding of the human condition and the problems we face. Its words offer encouragement and direction for how we can move forward beyond our trials and tribulations.

In our present moment of unrest and division, I have found great comfort in the words of the Apostle Paul in his letter to the church at Ephesus. For the sake of clarity and relevance, I often like to combine translations of the Bible and add my own paraphrase to Scriptural texts, which is a practice that religious teachers have engaged in since the earliest days of biblical teaching. What follows is my paraphrase of Paul's words in Ephesians 2:14–22:

> Jesus embodies for us what true peace looks like, for he was sent once and for all to take down the great wall of hatred and hostility that has divided us, so that we can be one.
>
> He gave up his life to bring an end to all the self-imposed and meaningless ideologies and laws that separated one people group from the people they consider outsiders. His desire was to create one new humanity from the two opposing groups, thus creating peace.
>
> Effectively the cross becomes God's means to put to death the hostility we create between ourselves once and for all so that we all may be reconciled together to God in this one new humanity. The Great Preacher of peace and love came for you, and His message reached those of you who were near and those who were far away. His message revealed to us that all people have access to God in one Spirit. And so you are no longer called outcasts, others, heretics, deplorable, unclean, or illegal immigrants but are full citizens with God's people, members of God's holy family, and residents of His household.

I have some breaking news: the same kind of divisions that Paul was talking about more than 1,900 years ago, are back in our day. Our nation is divided. Really, really divided. White people versus people of color. Rich versus poor. LGBTQ+ people versus Traditionalists. Trump supporters versus Democrats versus Moderates versus Progressives. And no matter where you stand today, no matter what direction you believe our nation is heading, all of us at some level are feeling a collective tension, a fear that something deeply distressing has been exposed in our world, and we are all wondering what exactly we can do about it.

For many of us, especially those with privilege, we have believed that our deepest divisions were healed. We believed that we had solved racism in the 1960s; that LGBTQ+ rights found its culmination in June 2015 when the Supreme Court legalized gay marriage; and that, despite differences in worldviews, we all were pretty much on the same page. Now, we know that nothing could be further from the truth. Families have been divided against themselves; entire sections of the nations have been divided against one another. This division is present in our churches, denominations, countries, and cities. Division is all around us, every single day. Many of us are also divided within ourselves.

When the veil is pulled back on reality and we are abruptly shaken out of our dream state, fear rises to the surface. And when fear emerges in our bodies, we get stupid. Literally. When fear is present, an area of our brain called the amygdala fires, and we lose the capacity to think rationally. We revert to our animalistic impulses, and we prepare to fight or to flee. When the amygdala fires, we begin acting in highly irrational ways.

We begin to build walls. We begin to segregate. We begin to demonize those who think, look, love, believe, vote, or act differently than us. We begin searching for a scapegoat, someone we can place the blame on for our problems and fears, and we begin to seek to exile them from our families, our communities, and our world. Fear causes us to do some truly dangerous, terrible things.

This is why the Scriptures says that fear and love are incompatible. That love expels fear. Because it's impossible to love, at least in the biblical sense, while we are acting like animals. Love requires higher levels of consciousness. It requires intentionality and hard work. It requires us to see our common humanity in all people and our interconnectedness to all of life. Love simply cannot manifest when we are reacting in fear.

As we're all well aware, in this moment of division and fear, many in our nation are acting irrationally. We are making choices and decisions, not out of love, not even out of rationality, but out of impulsive, often unjustifiable fear. Fear is what causes us to seek to build a wall to "keep out" those who we've been taught to believe are the cause of our problems with drugs and violence. Fear causes us to seek to ban and expel everyone who worships a different god or holds to a different worldview than we do. Fear is what causes us to posture ourselves for attack, ready to marginalize those who see things differently than we do—and that goes for all of us, regardless of what side of the ideological aisle we find ourselves on. Fear is what separates us, and love is the only thing that can bring us together.

In the portion of Ephesians that I paraphrased above, the Apostle Paul says that Jesus is the embodiment of what true peace looks like, because he was sent once and for all to tear down the wall of hostility that divided us so that we might be one. That sounds like a nice theological idea, but what does it actually mean?

Paul was writing to an ethnically and religiously divided people in Ephesus, a major costal city in Greece. The Jews believed that they were superior to the Gentiles, that their religion and customs made them more pure and more sophisticated. Likewise, the Gentiles saw the Jewish people as strange religious outcasts who didn't deserve to be fully integrated into society. So, when Paul felt called to bring the Gospel message beyond the Jewish people of Palestine to the rest of the world, they were faced with the need to confront their own prejudice and bias.

If they were going to be effective in spreading this message about Jesus, they knew they needed to go beyond their limited perspectives and beliefs, but to do that required confronting their fears about Gentiles and expanding their understanding of God's love, believing that it could and did extend beyond the Jewish people and was available to all people regardless of ethnicity or religious background. This was a radical notion then, and it still is today.

They were compelled to reach beyond themselves because they saw their rabbi, Jesus, constantly demonstrating this behavior. Jesus not only spoke to, but also befriended, ate with, and put his reputation on the line for all the people that many in his community wouldn't have touched with a ten-foot pole. Do you remember the time when Jesus invited himself over to Simeon the tax collectors' house for a meal? Or when a promiscuous woman met Jesus at a well, and they talked for a long while? Many religious leaders, and in fact, Jesus's own disciples, were beside themselves.

"You can't just hang around those kinds of people!" they snarled to each other. Yet Jesus insisted on breaking all the arbitrary rules that separated him from others. Jesus insisted on tearing down the walls that separated him from everyone else because he knew, and we know, that most of the walls we've created to separate us are imaginary, right? Tell me, really, what is the actual, tangible difference between a Democrat and a Republican as people? The differences are small and often trivial. But the similarities, namely, our common humanity, far outweigh any differences.

So, Jesus, in one fell swoop, destroys the imaginary walls that divide us. He shows us that all the prejudices and misconceptions that we continually use to make ourselves superior to others are all in our head. Because when Jesus is sitting at that table with Simeon, or at that well with the adulterous woman, or in the home of a Gentile, he is not experiencing them as tax collectors, adulterers, or Gentiles, but as human beings, as siblings, and manifestations of the same life and light that he himself partakes in. The same life and light that we *all* partake in.

You see, we are all *already* one. This is an inescapable reality. We are all made of the same substance and partake in the same fundamental nature. We live and move and have our being in the same universe. Any separation we experience is self-constructed and imaginary.

Amid our great cultural diversity, worldview diversity, and religious diversity, we're all already one at some fundamental level. But when you begin to mess with the walls, borders, and boundaries of separation that we create out of our fear, you're likely going to get some major blowback, because fear not only drives us to create walls, it also drives us to defend them at all costs. Fear gets us to believe the lie that we live in a world where everyone and everything is out to get us. That anyone who doesn't look like, believe like, or act like us is our enemy with a desire to harm us, even if 99 percent of the time there is no merit to that belief.

Paul tells us that Jesus ends up being executed precisely because of his work to tear down these imaginary walls. Both the religious and political officials of his day didn't like his constant subverting of cultural norms. They didn't like his message of love, unity, and forgiveness for all people, because his message was beginning to dissolve the false systems and structures that had been created to keep society running smoothly.

The incentive to maintain the status quo of division is the fact that once it's been fully accepted and integrated, it does, in fact, keep a society running smoothly. So, anyone who comes with a message that calls out our irrational fears and begins to chip away at our walls is bound to be faced with the threat of violence—because they're threating the equilibrium. And when social equilibrium is threatened, the threat must be removed. This is what happens to Jesus. It is what happened to Dr. Martin Luther King Jr. It is what happened to Nelson Mandela. It is what happened to the Dalai Lama. It happens to anyone who pulls back the veil and reveals the absurdity of our divisions. This kind of radical action is still needed in our day.

This is what Jesus's mission and ministry was all about—not preaching about heaven and hell but about being unified in our common humanity, which he claimed would bring justice and "heaven" to all. Notice what Paul says is necessary for this to become a reality:

> He gave up his life to bring an end to all of the self-imposed and meaningless ideologies and laws that separated one people group from the people they consider outsiders.

Jesus sought to reveal that all of the things that divided us were rooted in "self-imposed and meaningless laws and ideologies." Stuff that religious and political people thought up in their ivory towers of power and privilege but have absolutely nothing to do with the real things of life—justice, equality, peace, and love.

In our present moment we are being called by the Spirit to stop and consider the example of Jesus. The example that led him to subvert cultural norms, to tear down the walls of self-imposed standards that divide us, and to literally give up his own life to show us just how futile and dangerous humans can become when we act out of fear.

It's easy for us to think this message is for some other group of people. Surely this message doesn't apply to progressive, inclusive people of faith, does it? I believe that Jesus's message is probably more important for *us* than *anyone else*. In this moment of our collective history, even us progressives can too easily fall into the trap of fear leading to demonization. We might not be the ones calling for a wall between the United States and Mexico, but be assured that we are still building walls. Many of us have fallen into the trap of demonization where we see anyone who thinks, looks, acts, and believes differently than us as *the* problem for our society. We see them as archaic, bigoted hindrances to progress. We see them as out of touch and their existence as fundamentally dangerous. And we demonize them. We make them our "others," and tell ourselves the lie that if we just got rid of those people— the pro-lifers, the Trump supporters, the racists—*then* our country would finally be a place of progress and peace.

But we know, deep down, that's not the case. We know, deep down, that by demonizing entire groups of people, painting them with one broad brush and blaming them for all our problems, that we're only exacerbating the problems we face. Because our fear drives them to even more fear. We fall into their worst stereotypes about the "intolerant left," provoking a fear-based response from them. We crucify each other. We act out of our reptilian brains. We bring more destruction instead of the peace that we yearn for.

Today, the Spirit is calling us to examine our prejudice, our propensity to demonize, our failure to love, and the walls of our own building. And then I believe that the Spirit is calling us to do something bold—to *tear them down*. To change our perspective, seeing each person as a partaker in the Divine nature with us. We're being called to see each person as a unique combination of experiences, backgrounds, beliefs, and fears. To see each person as worthy of our time, our consideration, our empathy, and our love.

What would happen if instead of demonizing those who differ from us, we did what Jesus did? We took them for lunch? We went out for a drink? We made a point to get to know those who voted differently than us, seeking to understand their perspective? What if we worked to see them as beloved siblings, part of one human family? This doesn't mean that we must bypass or sugarcoat our disagreements. It doesn't mean we condone immoral behaviors. It just means that we connect as humans who all have a variety of lived experiences that lead us to our beliefs and perspectives. It invites us to hold the complexity of each person's beliefs and worldview without demonizing them or writing them off.

Perhaps if we did this, we would be able to lead our communities, our nation, and our world in a different direction. Perhaps, we would begin to experience the "one new humanity" that Jesus sought to create—beyond our meaningless divisions and fears. Perhaps, at last, we'd experience that more just and equal world that we all long for. Paul concludes the passage I paraphrased above from Ephesians 2 by writing these words in verse 17:

> The Great Preacher of peace and love came for you, and His message reached those of you who were near and those who were far away. His message revealed to us that all people have access to God in one Spirit. And so you are no longer called outcasts, others, heretics, deplorable,

overrated, unclean, or illegal immigrants but are full citizens with God's people, members of God's holy family, and residents of His household.

Jesus, our great preacher of peace and love has brought to us a message and example that calls us to move beyond impulsive fears; our propensity to judge; our addiction to scapegoating; and instead, to look at everyone as equal members of the human family. Our Scriptures teach that we all share one common humanity, one common light and spirit. No fellow human is truly an enemy. No human is truly an other.

When we take the risky, unpopular, uncomfortable path of Jesus and work to see the humanity in even our most despised enemies, we break open the floodgates of empathy and allow for the possibility of true and lasting progress. We begin doing something different and radical that truly has the potential to change the way things are for our collective good.

2

The Subversive Karma of God

The great prophet Justin Timberlake once sang, "What goes around, comes around." This principle has been echoed by many great teachers and philosophers throughout the centuries, not the least of which is the Apostle Paul who famously said, "God is not mocked. What you sow, you shall reap" (Galatians 6:7).

While this statement is not always true—sometimes, really bad people do seem to get away with doing bad, and really good people seem to have terrible things happen to them—there seems to be a general level of truthfulness to this claim.

When we live in a way that is kind, compassionate, and generous to others, we often receive the same behavior aimed back at us. Likewise, if we are rude, critical, and hard on everyone around us, it is likely that we will receive negative attitudes directed toward us as well. In my experience, this principle even goes beyond our actions, but it extends to our attitudes.

I often talk about the power of "coming out" for LGBTQ+ individuals. In the coming out experience, there is a deep truth that when people live in fear of some part of who they are and feel like they must suppress or hide some fundamental part of themselves, they often will experience the sour fruits of that fear. That is not to say that it's not necessary for some people to hide their LGBTQ+ identities to remain safe sometimes, but rather that repression always has a net negative effect on their lives.

On the flip side, the more we value and are freed to live in authenticity—not feeling like we need to put on a show for anyone but are happy to show up with our full selves to every area of our lives—we will usually reap the rewards of living with such authenticity.

Consider the story of Esther from the Hebrew Bible. It is a story about a young Jewish woman who finds herself chosen as the new wife of a king who has been influenced by his racist advisers to exterminate the Jewish people in his kingdom. Esther's uncle, Mordecai, tells her to hide her Jewish identity. It is the only way that she can be safe and is perhaps the only way that she can eventually help influence the king to save her people.

Early in the text, we read the story of how the king's adviser, Haman, plotted to have Mordecai, Esther's Jewish uncle, killed. Instead of carrying out Haman's desire, the king decides to reward Mordecai because he has acted with integrity—warning the king about a plot to assassinate him—honoring Mordecai in front of the whole city. Even in that moment, we see a bit of the truth of this karma principle. Mordecai acted righteously—even toward the king, his enemy who had just decreed that he and his people should be killed—and his righteous act ended up subverting the evil plot of Haman. Mordecai was honored, and Haman walked away in shame.

The story continues with Queen Esther approaching the king and Haman, with a bold request—for the king to not destroy her people. The king reacts with surprise, saying, "Who is the one who has dared to do such a thing?" not realizing he's been tricked into making such a decree by Haman. Esther immediately reveals what Haman has done—seeking to exterminate her people and even plotting to kill her uncle Mordecai simply because he was Jewish. The king is incensed—he demands that a pole be set up and Haman killed immediately and publicly in the same way Haman had planned for Mordecai to be killed.

Following Haman's execution, the king gives Esther everything Haman owned, and Esther gives all the possessions to Mordecai. Esther again appeals to the king to reverse more of his orders, snuck in by Haman, that prevented Jews from defending themselves. The king agreed to reverse the orders and sends Mordecai to share the news with the Jews throughout Susa. They rejoice and celebrate for days on end. When enemies eventually do come to attack the Jews, they fight and win the battle against those who hated them. King is impressed and goes back to Esther, asking what else she might want. She asks that Haman's sons who were killed in the battle be stuck on poles as well, so everyone can see them. When the king honors this final request, a period of rest and celebration ensues for the Jewish people who rejoiced at their resilience and overcoming of their enemies.

Haman, the evil, racist adviser to King Xerxes reaps what he had sown. His racism had led him to convince the king to order that all the Jews in his empire be killed, but because of Esther and Mordecai's bravery and willingness to live authentically and speak up for what was right, Haman's evil plot was yet again exposed. The very death he was planning for Mordecai fell upon him and his entire family.

This myth of profound bravery and living authentically is the basis of the Jewish feast of Purim, a time when the Jewish people come together to celebrate their collective resilience and ability to overcome the constant threats leveled against them. Reflecting on the story of Esther and the feast of Purim, Rabbi Nathan Lopez Cardozo writes:

> Jews have been an ever-dying people that never died. They have experienced a continuous resurrection, like the dry bones that Ezekiel saw in the valley. This has become the sine qua non of every Jew. It is the mystery of the hidden miracle of survival in the face of overwhelming

destruction. Our refusal to surrender has turned our story into one long, unending Purim tale.[1]

This statement is profoundly true: it's why the Jewish author of Esther originally penned this tale—because while these events may not have been literally true (scholars agree that the Book of Esther is a myth), the broad narrative is deeply true for the Jewish people. Throughout history, they've constantly faced hatred and destruction simply based on their identity, and through their resilience, they have overcome. As Rabbi Cardozo writes, they are the "ever-dying people that never died." That's a beautiful and heartbreaking statement, isn't it?

The same could be said of many other minority groups. Across this nation, Black folks are an "ever dying people that never died." They have faced racism and violence simply because of who they are, and yet even in the face of such a threat, they persist, resist, and find *joy*. This is where the African American spiritual emerges from—those beautiful, hope-filled songs that were originally sung by enslaved peoples. They faced their oppression with an eye toward the justice of God and a better day.

They sang, "Go down, Moses, way down to Egypt land. Tell ole' Pharaoh, let my people go." They sang, "Swing low, sweet chariot. Comin' for to carry me home. I looked over Jordan and what did I see but a band of angels comin' after me. Comin' for to carry me home." The spirit of Purim is embodied in these songs. The spirit of strength in the face of injustice. Of hope in the face of hopelessness. Of a determination to find joy knowing that it is indeed true, "What you sow, you shall reap." These are not songs of submission. They are not songs of merely accepting their circumstances. They are songs that echo the deep truth of the universe that reverberates in the hearts of all people—that as the Hebrew Prophet Amos wrote—some day "Justice will roll on like a river, righteousness like a never-failing stream!"

The message of Purim and the message of the Book of Esther is this: in the face of evil and injustice, in the face of hatred and fear, keep living authentically, exposing the darkness, and fighting for a better world. It's a message that calls us to keep trusting that God's law, written in the fabric of the universe is true: righteousness will prevail. The so-called last in society *will* be made first. A day of reckoning will come. God *will* vindicate all who have been on the receiving end of injustice. It's a call to remember that the Hamans of the world *will* meet their demise and that the Esthers and Mordecais *will* have the last word. Because of this hope, we can have joy as we fight for a more just and equal world. And our joy is often one of the most powerful weapons to agitate the oppressor. This is true on a large, societal scale and on the individual level.

We may face those who seek to take advantage of us and do wrong to us. The lesson of the Book of Esther is *not* that we should just "take it" and trust God. That's a false and abusive teaching that far too many religious leaders have promulgated. Suffering is never a requirement of God. At the same time, the promise of the Gospel is that suffering can be redeemed. If you have suffered injustice, unfairness, or wrongdoing at the hands of another, God can bring healing and redemption. As the writer of Genesis wrote, "You intended to harm me, but God intended it for good to accomplish what is now being done, the saving of many lives." God can use evil to make you resilient, stronger, and more able to resist and defeat evil in your life in the future.

The story of Esther provides a number of lessons for all people who have ever experienced injustice. First, the story teaches that we must choose to live authentically in the face of evil. We cannot allow the hatred or fear of others to cause us to live in closets of shame or fear. Second, the story teaches that we must be bold and courageous, willing to speak truth to power even if it costs us. This is what Esther does when she approaches the king and asks for her people to be saved. Third, the story teaches us that we must celebrate righteousness and justice, and constantly remind ourselves of stories and times when we have overcome, to have faith and strength that we can and will overcome again. And finally, it reminds us that we must remember that God is at work in our world, and that even when we may not see God's hand or feel God's presence, we're called to have faith that the Spirit is moving, empowering, and working to bring about righteousness. As Martin Luther King Jr. famously declared,

> Evil may so shape events that Caesar will occupy a palace and Christ a cross, but that same Christ will rise up and split history into A.D. and B.C., so that even the life of Caesar must be dated by his name. Yes, "the arc of the moral universe is long, but it bends toward justice."[2]

There will be moments, like the one we are in now, where evil may seem to be winning. Where injustice, hatred, racism, prejudice seem to be on the rise. There may be moments when the innocent and righteous face crucifixion while the unjust occupy palaces of power. But through the power of God and the resilience of all who are committed to living according to the way of justice, equity, righteousness, and peace, there is the hope of redemption. There is the hope that as long as we continue to fight in the power of God, for God's will, against the powers and principalities that are at work to bring destruction, the arc of our universe will continue its long journey toward justice.

It is my prayer that we will awaken from our complacency and indifference. From our childish faith that simply presumes justice will happen because God is in control to a faith that realizes that God has placed the responsibility for justice *in our hands*. That those of us who have influence, wealth, power, or privilege will commit to using their privilege to establish justice for those who do not. And when we bring these forces together, the same may be said about us that is written about Mordecai in the final verse of the book of Esther: "He sought the good of his people and interceded for the welfare of all his descendants." This is our call.

3

Let's Talk about Inner Reformation

We are in a moment of unprecedented change. On every continent, political upheaval, social unrest, and religious turmoil are beginning to reach a boiling point.

A number of prophetic voices have risen up and spoken about this moment, a period that is coming in which everything about how we live, think, believe, and see the world will be challenged and transformed. These seers and prophets looked at the signs and drew on the wisdom and insight of a long line of saints before them, who had called for deconstruction, expansion, reformation, and renewal of how we see and live.

Among the most influential of these saints to inspire today's prophets are Francis of Assisi and Martin Luther. Both of them unwittingly stepped into prophetic roles in their time that fundamentally shifted the way the church and society would function for good, and today we would do well to lean back and listen to their wisdom and practice as we stand on the brink of a new reformation of Spirit.

Jesus taught us that all true and substantial transformation in the world must first begin with the hearts of those who will bring about that transformation. This is what he meant when he said that the Kingdom of God was within us, and then prayed for us to manifest the Kingdom of God on earth, in the world, as it is in that heavenly realm of the Eternal Soul. This is the fundamental rhythm of Christianity. Inward transformation begets outward renewal. We are filled up and then we are poured out. This is what our central act of worship, the Eucharist, embodies—first receiving from God the gift of grace, then being called to go out into the world, breaking open our bodies, and pouring out our lives for the good of friends, neighbors, and enemies. If we are to be active and effective participants in this new reformation that God is bringing about in our day, we must allow the wild, untamable Spirit of God to begin that reformation in our lives.

But what does this look like? How do we open ourselves up to allow the Spirit to have her way in our souls? This is the question that every faithful seeker of God has wrestled with, and is a question that Francis and Luther spent much time exploring.

For St. Francis, the initial moment of soul reformation was sparked during two personal moments of conviction. First, feeling lost and dissatisfied with the life he was living as a soldier, Francis found himself praying in the forsaken chapel of San Damiano in Assisi. In the midst of his prayer, he hears that still small voice of God within himself say, "Go, Francis, and repair my house which you see has fallen into ruin." Francis hears these words and takes them literally, and dedicates himself to repairing the run-down chapel that he found himself in.

Isn't it funny how when we receive a prompting from the Spirit, we often interpret it in the most literal terms so as to avoid its much broader, and more costly ramifications? Francis repaired the chapel of San Damiano, but the Spirit's prompting was about more than that. It was a call to repair the church, which had fallen far from the true heart of the Gospel that Jesus proclaimed and embodied. Instead of focusing on the manifestation of the Kingdom of God within the individual and in the world, the church had become focused on piety, on religious orders, on power and other vain pursuits that had little to do with the inner and outer journey of redemption. The church had indeed fallen into ruin, and God was prompting Francis to do something about it.

The second moment of transformation for Francis was just a little while later, when, with the help of a local priest, he opened the Bible looking for wisdom and landed on Jesus's teaching in Matthew 10:9, proclaiming that the Kingdom of Heaven was within and upon his disciples, and that in the pursuit and proclamation of the Kingdom, his disciples needed no earthly belongings. Francis, again, taking these words literally, throws away all of his possessions and immediately embarks on a missionary journey throughout the Italian countryside, proclaiming this message of simplicity, love, and grace, which is the true heart of the Gospel of Christ. From this moment onward, Francis began to gain followers, those who had grown disillusioned with the principles and practices of most religion and sought a more Christ-like way of seeing and being in the world. Within a short period of time, Francis developed a rule of life that would form the basis of one of the most famous, revolutionary, and important monastic orders in the history of Christianity, the Franciscans.

Similarly, for Martin Luther, his initial moment of transformation came after entering into monastic life and growing deeply disillusioned by the practices of the church. One day, while reading Psalm 22 where the psalmist proclaims, "My God, My God, why have you abandoned me?" Luther recognized that disillusionment with God and the institutions that represent God is as old a spiritual experience as salvation itself. Luther continued to study and seek God in spite of his sense of angst and distance from the Divine, and two years later when reading the words of the Apostle Paul when he wrote "the just shall live by faith" in his letter to the Romans, Luther realized that salvation had little to do with believing the right doctrines or conforming to the traditions of the church, but rather on simple faith and openness to God.

This moment of hearing the voice of Spirit through the words of Scripture ignited a flame within Luther that caused him to begin to question and ultimately call for the overturning of the unjust teachings and traditions that the church had adopted. Within a few years of this awakening, Luther nailed his now infamous

"Ninety-Five Theses" to the door of a cathedral in his town, and called for Christianity to repent of and reform its greedy and un-Christlike teaching and practices, which ignited the movement that become known as the Protestant Reformation.

These three moments represent a number of principles of inner reformation that each of us must awaken to if we are to be of any use to the Spirit in her present work of transforming the world.

Principle 1: Awareness of Spirit's Promptings

Being aware. Hearing, in order to respond, to the voice of the Spirit of God. This is the first principle we see in these great examples from the past.

God is always speaking. The Scriptures proclaim that Christ is *"living and active"* (Hebrews 4:12), always speaking with penetrating insights into our present circumstances. Yet so much of modern Christianity has adopted a belief that the Spirit is silent and that we should not expect to hear the voice of God beyond what was revealed in ancient Scriptures or proclaimed by the Great Tradition. What we will see is that for both Francis and Luther, it was disillusionment with this image of a stagnant God that they were first forced to wrestle with and reject that prompted their inner and outer work for reformation.

If the Spirit of God is silent and has spoken all that she needs to say, then we have nothing to do. Our only work is to seek to conform to the knowledge that we have already been taught. Thinking is not necessary, only unquestioning obedience to the authorities that have supposedly been instituted by God. Wouldn't this make the leaders of our religious institutions gleeful?

The problem is that the way of Jesus flies directly in the face of such a teaching. Jesus spent his entire ministry disrupting the traditions of humans; questioning the authority and interpretation of Scripture that was being promoted by the religious elite; and speaking new, fresh words generated by the Spirit. Not only did Jesus himself do this, but he taught that his disciples for generations to come should expect to do the same and greater things than he did.

Jesus taught that his life and teachings were only the tip of the iceberg of reformation and renewal. He proclaimed that he had *many more things to teach the world,* more than his disciples *could now bear.* It is at that point that he promises the outpouring of the Holy Spirit whose job would be to *continue to lead us into all truth.*

In other words, the Spirit of God, which Jesus said in John 3:8 is as *wild and unpredictable as the wind,* was going to be sent to dwell in the hearts of humanity with the express mission of leading us to greater truth and toward a more complete manifestation of the Kingdom of God in our lives and on earth as it is in heaven.

But to *hear* the voice of the Spirit, we must first be aware, awake, and expecting the Spirit to speak. Clearly, both Francis and Luther in their desperation and disillusionment with Christianity found themselves longing for a sign, a word, a symbol from God to lead them on the true path to awakening and salvation. For both men, the Spirit spoke in unexpected times and through unexpected means and called them to challenge and change the way faith was being expressed, first within their own personal lives and then in the rest of the world.

Both men embodied openness to the Spirit and a willingness to respond to *whatever* she may have to say, no matter how radical or controversial. They didn't fear finding themselves exiled as "heretics" or cut off from the structures of privilege and power because they sought something deeper than religious or social accolades—they sought union with Christ and the experience of his Kingdom in their lives and on earth.

This openness and attentiveness to hear what the Spirit might be speaking is the fundamental posture of reformation. If we are to experience an inner revolution that has power to bring about the liberation and salvation that Jesus embodied, we must first discipline ourselves to be aware and alert for the Spirit of God to speak, and be ready to obey regardless of the personal cost.

Principle 2: Spiritual Discipline

Discipline is probably the most apparent principle of spiritual awakening and yet is also the hardest to do. Unceasing spiritual discipline. Both Francis and Luther were committed to being *disciplined* in their pursuit of God. Francis was driven to the point of desperation because of the dissatisfaction he experienced in his life and was driven to fervent prayer and contemplation. Similarly, Luther felt utterly disconnected from God and disillusioned with the church, yet continued to pray, study, and seek after the experience of Christ for years before he finally heard the Spirit speak through the words of Scripture and was emboldened to begin his work of renewal.

The journey of both men mirrors the spiritual journey of ordinary people. When we move beyond the mythologizing of their lives and spiritual journeys and focus on the raw biographical knowledge we have of them, we find two individuals who found themselves fed up with the shallowness of how they were living and disillusioned by the hollowness of the Christianity they experienced, and therefore they were drawn to seek God through intense personal devotion and discipline. The path of discipline and devotion is the *only* path that leads to inner transformation.

In nearly every spiritual tradition, it is the path of prayer, meditation, and contemplation that is prescribed as the path that leads to eternal and abundant life. And in every generation, there are those who seek to shortcut the path of contemplation and dilute the command to be disciplined to taste salvation, leading to the sort of useless religion that both Francis and Luther railed against.

In our day, there are more shallow religion and hollow self-help teachings that promise to give us a better life with great speed and little work. There are drugs to take, intensive retreats to go on, and mindless practices to adopt that promise to help us experience a life of depth. *None* of these paths work. None of them ultimately lead to the abundant life that Jesus proclaimed, and none give us the fuel we need to be agents of redemption in the world around us. Any path that is divorced from consistent spiritual discipline can only give us a momentary spiritual high, a glimpse of the experience of salvation, before painfully dropping us back on the dusty ground of meaninglessness and hopelessness.

If we are to experience true soul reformation that leads to societal transformation, we must commit ourselves to consistent spiritual discipline. We may go days, months, or years without experiencing anything substantial, but we can be assured that with every meditation or moment of contemplation, we are expanding our capacity to receive from God and amplifying the voice of our soul in the work of global transformation.

Principle 3: Sacrificial Obedience

The third principle of inner reformation we can learn from Francis and Luther is sacrificial and courageous obedience. Upon hearing the word of the Spirit through their prayerful obedience, both Francis and Luther respond to the Spirit's leading with sacrifice and courage. This, it seems, has been the very definition of faith from the very beginning. In Genesis, we are told of the call of Abram, who hears the voice of the Spirit calling him to leave his land and family and trust God's leading to a new, unknown land. The writer of Genesis says, immediately following the text of the Spirit's call in Genesis 12:4, "thus Abram departed, just as the Lord had told him." It is this moment that becomes the sign of true faith, lauded throughout the rest of the Hebrew Bible and in the New Testament.

Both Francis and Luther follow in this same path, hearing the Spirit and responding without hesitation to do that which they are called to do. Francis strips off his expensive clothes and renounces his father and family wealth in the town square, and immediately sets out to preach the Gospel to lepers and outcasts. Luther is awakened to the profound simplicity of the path of faith through the grace of God, apart from works, and responds by speaking out boldly against the very institution to which he belongs. Both actions required tremendous courage and a willingness to sacrifice comfort, privilege, and power for the good of the world.

This courageous, sacrificial faith is at the heart of any true awakening. Courage and sacrifice require that we live with open hands, ready to work hard to manifest the more beautiful world that God desires, while also recognizing that we are but channels of the Divine and that all that we might accomplish isn't ours but belongs only to God, and therefore we are willing to give our all and sacrifice everything in courageous confidence that God will have the last word in the end.

Often, the sacrifice that comes as a result of our courageous obedience is painful to our ego. At the end of his life, stricken with illness, Francis was pushed to the edge of the religious order that he founded and was forced to resign as its leader. Luther's own spiritual movement was morphed into a violent protest against the church, which ultimately resulted in Luther being excommunicated from the church and forced into hiding for many years to avoid being imprisoned. Both men suffered greatly for their obedience to the Spirit's nudge in their lives, but their sacrifices galvanized the reforming work that God was doing in and through them.

As we seek to allow the Spirit of God to reform our lives from the inside out, we must be obedient, courageous, and sacrificial. We must respond to the prompting of the Spirit without fear and with complete faith that God is with us and in us and will bring us to the day of redemption, as the Apostle Paul proclaims. Sometimes the path of sacrifice will lead us into the valleys of suffering and loss, but even there, we can be assured that God's rod and staff will guide and comfort us, as the familiar Psalm 23 puts it.

Nearly every spiritual tradition teaches that sacrifice and suffering precede full awakening. This does not mean that we must search for suffering, but rather that when we live courageously and obediently, suffering will emerge as a season that we must endure in order to be refined and to put to death the ego.

Principle 4: Embrace Simplicity

The fourth principle is to embrace humility, nonjudgment, and simplicity. Both Francis and Luther were raised in religious systems that valued complexity, austerity, and gaudiness.

All religious systems have the tendency to move toward judgmentalism, hypercomplexity, and sheer egoic pride. Our doctrines begin to favor us versus them, roles and levels of spiritual maturity emerge in the form of systems that privilege a few and oppress many, and we become so caught up in defining the indefinable and being proud of how much we know. This is the kind of Christianity that both Francis and Luther found themselves in, and it was this tangled web of shallow religiosity that resulted in their profound disillusionment and dissatisfaction.

Both men found themselves on the top of the religious and social hierarchy early on, and much like the story of Siddhartha Gautama (who became known as the Buddha), they were protected from suffering in the world that resulted from religious and social systems that privileged them over others. But as is often the case, the privileged life loses its luster and is revealed to be vapid and lacking substance, and both men found themselves in a posture of seeking more meaning.

When Francis awakened to his simple path, he sold everything he had and went to preach among the poor and marginalized. Through this process, he experienced the gradual death of his false self and moved from a posture of judgment to nonjudgment, recognizing that he was interconnected with and related to all created things. No one was above another, and all were equally loved and embraced by God.

When Luther awakened to the potency of God's grace and the simplicity of salvation by faith, he rejected creeds and hierarchies in order to preach a Gospel message that was truly *good news of great joy for all people*. A message that freed the poor from exploitation and held the mirror of Jesus in the faces of the religious hierarchy, revealing the injustices. His goal was never to

leave the church but to call it back to the simpler path of salvation that Jesus demonstrated, beyond the greed and theological
complexity that the church had embraced as holy.

Neither man sought to gain large followings. Both only
sought to be obedient to the Spirit and faithful to their convictions. But as they embraced the simple, humble, nonjudg-
mental way of Jesus, others noticed and were drawn to them.
By living in the joy that comes from simplicity and humility,
they put the church to shame and drew all those who were
feeling the shallowness and incongruence of the institutional-
ized religion with that of the life and teachings of Jesus, who
refused to fall into the practices of the religious leaders of his
day who preached condemnation and conformity, but instead
proclaimed that the peace of God was available to all and
that all could participate in the Kingdom of God through the
simple realization of the grace and mercy that was already
encompassing each one of us.

If we are to allow the Spirit of God to bring about a reformation of Spirit within us, we must abandon our attachment to
things, to power, to wealth, and instead, embrace the simple path
that Jesus embodied; to recognize the siblinghood we share with
all people and all created things; and to live a life infused with
grace, acknowledging the journey that each and every person is
on toward reformation and redemption.

When we embody these traits, we become beacons of the
light of Christ, and many will be drawn to the rhythm that we
live our lives to. This is the best evangelism one could hope for,
and the path that Jesus himself favored. Our inner peace begets
outer peace; our inner simplicity begets outer simplicity; and
when we leave behind toxic theologies that teach of God's judgment on those who don't conform, we experience the liberation
that comes from knowing that God's posture toward us is only
and always love, and that nothing can separate us from that
fundamental reality.

Principle 5: Incarnational Living

Then there is the necessity of living an incarnational and ordinary life. At the heart of the Christian story is the belief that in the person of Jesus, God became a human, put on flesh, and made God's dwelling among us. Jesus reveals to us God with dirt under his fingernails, a God who is with us on the turbulent trails of life. The incarnation also therefore reveals the posture that followers of Jesus are called to embrace—being in the world but not of the world, as John 15:19 puts it, which means that we are to live fully immersed in, engaged with, and a part of the culture, while embracing a radically subversive way of living in the midst of the world.

Francis and Luther understood this well. While both explored and experimented with monastic life, both ultimately ended up understanding the importance of living as *monks in the world*, those who embraced the contemplative, simple, gracious lifestyle of Jesus while still being *ordinary folk* who could be found hanging around town, drinking a beer, or having a meal with friends. To live in step with the example of Jesus, they could not just separate themselves and live confined to a cloister but must experience God in and through *other people*. If their vision of reformation was going to have an impact, it must be accessible to the ordinary person living an ordinary life.

The church had done a great job creating a class system that separated the "most holy," namely, clergy and ecclesial leaders, from the rest of society, perpetuating a fundamentally anti-Christian teaching that God was only accessible (or at least more readily accessible) to certain people who had studied theology, been ordained, or had power and wealth. This flew in the face of Jesus and fostered the idea among the lower classes that they could not access God and were not prioritized by the church.

This split was a reflection of the gnostic tendencies of Christianity to separate the spirit from the physical, the clean from the unclean, saved from unsaved. But the path that Jesus embodied and that Francis and Luther recovered was the holistic path that saw all of life as spiritual, saw all people as equally filled with the Spirit of God, and therefore, the entire world stood on a level playing field before God. Everyone "*lived and moved and had their being* in God" (Acts 17:28), everyone mattered to God, and everyone had unlimited access to God at all times. This was the heart of the good news of Christianity and yet was the furthest thing from what the church was teaching.

To be a Christian was to live among others, for others. As Francis's associate St. Clare once wrote in a letter to Francis, "God did not call you only for yourself, but the good of others." The spiritually rooted life, then, was not for hiding away in endless contemplation but was lived in public, marked by good works rooted in deep faith. The incarnational thrust of Christianity called both men out of the monastery and into the town center, bringing about social and spiritual reformation through living ordinary lives rooted in a vibrant connection to the Spirit.

If we are to follow their example, we must live our faith out loud. It must not be a subset of our life, but the ground of all we do. We must refuse the temptation to disconnect and see ourselves as set apart, and instead live in a way that helps others see that the ground of their being is also God and that every aspect of their lives are infused with Spirit.

Principle 6: Have Fun

I think the sixth and final principle of inner spiritual reformation is to always make room for fun. If any two figures in Christian history knew the importance of lightheartedness and fun, it was Francis and Luther. Prior to his enlightenment, Francis was known for throwing lavish parties and having a good time with friends out on the town. Even after dedicating his life to the simple way of Jesus, he continued to embrace a lighthearted, carefree attitude as he engaged in dancing, playing, and enjoying the company of friends. Luther also came to this realization, and often was seen enjoying a pint or three at the local pub in his hometown of Wittenberg.

Both men realized that the greatest threat to spiritual growth and flourishing was to take oneself too seriously. After all, we're talking about two men dedicated to following in the path of the renegade rabbi from Nazareth who himself had a reputation for partying and having a good time. In this way, childish lightheartedness is important. It helps us to keep in perspective the reality that we are finite and that while we have much power and are cared for eternally by our Creator, we are nonetheless incapable of directing our own paths. We are invited to follow in the way of the untamable and wild Spirit, and hold everything loosely, allowing the mighty currents of Spirit to take us wherever they may lead.

This lack of control and humility naturally gives birth to humor and fun. When we are dead set on appeasing God, earning salvation, or saving ourselves, we end up in a path of anxiety, stress, and begrudgery. Life is meant to be enjoyed and explored, and in the midst of the fun, our souls will soar and stretch. The Indian spiritual teacher Osho writes, *"God is always joking! Look at your own life—it is a joke. Look at other people's lives and you will find jokes and jokes and jokes. Seriousness is illness. Seriousness has nothing spiritual about it. Spirituality is laughter. Spirituality is joy. Spirituality is fun."*[3]

Isn't it interesting that the idea of living a spiritually disciplined life is often conceived of as an austere, serious reality, when those who are most enlightened, most awakened, are often the most lighthearted? Have you ever watched a video of the Dalai Lama and the late Desmond Tutu together? They were constantly laughing, joking, and tickling each other. To be deeply spiritual, united to God, is to be one who can lean back fully into the flow of life and let the river take you where it desires, with your only task being to enjoy the ride. This is the beauty of true spirituality: it happens to us, for us, and through us. We don't have to do *anything* to make it happen. Only enjoy it. This is also the beauty and power of grace. So, make time for fun, laugh a little, and tell stories. Balance your silence with laughter, your seriousness with smiles. When we live happier lives, we live healthier and more spiritually balanced lives.

A New Reformation

None of these principles I have shared are revolutionary or profound—they are not meant to be. Spirituality is not a way of life; it is life itself. We are all living a rule of life, the question is whether or not we are aware of it and intentional about it. Life isn't meant to be strenuous, but simple. We're not looking for an extraordinary spiritual awakening, but rather the waking up of spirit that takes place in our ordinary, day-to-day life. It is not the dramatic, ecstatic, and extreme that actually lead to lasting and sustainable transformation, but the rhythmic, constant, simple, disciplined practices that ground us and center us.

I believe that the Spirit is calling us all to be agents of reformation in this new era. But any outer reformation that may come must first begin as inner reformation. May we be open to the reformation of Spirit that you are calling us to, Holy Spirit. May we heed your call, carry forth the flame of your refining fire, and be transformed for the glory and redemption of the world.

4

The Jesus You Never Knew

To be a Christian is to follow Jesus, whose life and teachings are found in the four Gospels at the beginning of the New Testament. But so much of what modern Christians think about Jesus comes not from these biblical texts, but from pictures painted by our cultural imagination.

For instance, the predominant image of Jesus in paintings around the world for the last one thousand years has been of a White, European man. Yet we know that Jesus—a Jewish Palestinian—looks nothing like this. Similarly, much of the theology developed in churches about who Jesus is bears very little resemblance to the Jesus we find in the Gospels, which are our only reliable historical accounts of Jesus life. The fact is, much of what we think we know about Jesus bears little resemblance to the actual Jesus of Scripture, just as much of the theology that bears the name of Jesus didn't originate from his lips.

One of the most obvious things that Christians forget when thinking about Jesus is that he was a human being, just like you and me. On a human level, Jesus wasn't unique at all. In first-century Palestine, Jesus wouldn't have stood out as anything special for much of his life. He went to school like all the other kids. He played the same games. As he grew, he worked the same kind of jobs that others did. He ate the same food. He went to the same parties. He joined the same clubs. By and large, Jesus was a regular human being, and if Jesus was present on earth today, he would be a regular, twenty-first-century human.

Yet, the image of Jesus that so many of us have embraced and imagined is one that makes Jesus wholly different than us. It sees him as a god, like in ancient pagan religions, that hovered a foot off the ground and walked around with a halo on his head.

Yet the Jesus of the Bible is largely portrayed as a regular human being—he looked like us, acted like us, got hurt, enjoyed good food and drink, had friends, and got annoyed with them. He was thoroughly human. But why is it so important to emphasize this point? Because if we fail to understand just how human Jesus was, then we fail to understand the entire purpose of the incarnation.

You see, I believe that the reason God became a human being was twofold. First, Jesus needed to learn what it was like to be human to empathize with the human condition. And second, Jesus needed to show us that it was possible to live the whole and holy life that God intended for us.

According to Christian theology, our Creator loves us so much that they* decided to come to the world that they created, to put on flesh, to become a human in space and time—with all the limitations of being human—so that they could experience what it was like to live in a world infected by sin. This tells us something crucial and comforting about the nature of God—that God is not some distant force that set the world in motion and abandoned us. God isn't a Divine dictator who desires to pour judgment out on us for doing wrong. No, the God revealed in Jesus is a God who cares so deeply about us that they wanted to walk with us, to experience the world with all its hardships and

---

* In an era where there is increasing clarity around how we speak about God in relation to gender, I think it's important to remember that in Genesis Chapters 1 and 2, the Hebrew word to describe God is plural, and thus merits a plural pronoun, rather than a singular gendered pronoun especially in reference to these texts.

struggles, and to experience even the deepest pain—suffering and death—so that they could truly be with us and understand our suffering.

That truth is profoundly beautiful. Especially when we find ourselves in times when the entire world, collective humanity, is suffering. In moments like this, the image of Jesus shows us that God is with us, that God is with those suffering in hospitals, that God is with us isolated in our homes and riddled with fear of the uncertainty of the future. God can empathize with us. God knows what it is like. And God deeply cares for us.

The second reason is that Jesus, being a human, shows us that it is in fact possible to live a life according to God's will. That the holy life God created us to live, the values and principles that Jesus embodied, are in fact possible for us to live out as well. They're not for superhumans. The beatitudes and the Sermon on the Mount are well within our ability to obey. That's not to say that it's easy—even Jesus shows us that he struggled to obey all the God desired for him—but it *is* totally possible to live a whole and holy life.

As I have studied the life of Jesus over the past decade, I've come to see five aspects of the humanity of Jesus that can teach us profound lessons about the human experience. Some of these aspects of Jesus may be familiar to you, and some may not. But as we explore the evidence of Jesus's humanity from the Scriptures, it's my hope that we find encouragement to dig deeper into our relationship with Christ and our commitment to follow in his path.

First, like all humans, Jesus struggled with temptation to do wrong. Therefore, we can overcome temptation. Each Lent, Christians around the world commemorate the forty days that Jesus went into the Judean Wilderness to fast and pray, where he was tempted by the devil to do all sorts of evil. Why would the Gospel writers include such a troubling notion—that Jesus was profoundly tempted to do evil? I believe the writer of Hebrews sums it up best when they write, "we do not have a High Priest who cannot sympathize with our weaknesses, but was in all points tempted as we are, yet without sin" (Hebrews 4:15). Here the writer tells us that our High Priest, which is Jewish Messianic language, is able to "sympathize with our weakness" because he was tempted in *"all points, just as we are."*

For those who have an overly Divine image of Jesus, this point may be uncomfortable to think about. If true, this means that Jesus, like any human, was tempted to do all sorts of wrong. Jesus was tempted to lie. He was tempted to hurt others. He was tempted to sexually objectify others. He was tempted to cheat on his taxes. In "every way," Jesus was tempted like you and me. Jesus knows the struggle that we all face to live a good, a moral life. He knows how hard it is to always be honest. He knows, personally, how hard it is to have self-control. He knows, personally, how hard it is to be kind to that person that just grates on your nerves. He experienced it. He struggled with it. He really considered giving in to it.

And yet.

He overcame these temptations. We see this most profoundly as he faced his death. In the account of Jesus's final moments, before he was arrested, the Gospels tell us that he wrestled with God. He begged God to find another way, to get him out of the horrifying circumstances he was facing. Yet ultimately, he proclaims the words: "Not my will, but yours be done" (Luke 22:44).

Jesus shows us that it's not easy to follow God's way in a world infected with sin and brokenness, but it is possible. He shows us that it's not wrong to be tempted. It's not wrong to struggle. It's not wrong to have to fight within your mind to do what you know is right and good. He shows us that it is possible to do what is right—to train ourselves to live according to God's values. It is possible to overcome temptation and live a whole life like God created us to live. Jesus, the human, struggled with temptation. But he overcame. Thus showing us that we can, too.

The second thing we learn from the Gospels about the human Jesus is that Jesus grew and developed spiritually. Therefore, spiritual growth takes practice. Ancient Christians developed a lot of fun myths about Jesus—some of them portray Jesus as being born with the full spiritual development and intellect of the thirty-year-old man we experience in the Gospels. They often told stories of the infant Jesus getting up and running around teaching people, performing miracles, and frankly, being a snarky wise guy. But these accounts are nothing more than mythology, because if Jesus was a human like us, he grew and developed like we do. In fact, the Canonical Gospels, which tell us almost nothing about Jesus's childhood, simply give us this brief summary of the first twelve years of his life: "And Jesus grew in wisdom and stature, and in favor with God and men" (Luke 2:52).

Jesus grew in wisdom and stature—a phrase meaning he grew in his mental capacities and physically. He grew in favor with God and men—a phrase indicating he spiritually matured and matured as a respectable member of his society. This means, quite simply, that Jesus had to learn. He had to have spiritual discipline and practice growing in spiritual depth with God. Jesus didn't come out of the womb with wisdom and knowledge. Like all of us, he had to learn, grow, and take time to evolve into the man he became.

Now, many might be thinking—well wait, doesn't Christian theology proclaim that Jesus is God? How could he not know something? What would he need to learn? That's a fair question. The answer from our Christian tradition is that God, in Jesus, chose to limit themselves. They wanted to experience what humanity truly experienced, which means that God in Jesus chose not to know all things. Not to have infinite wisdom. Thus, God in Jesus learned just like we do.

We see this in Jesus's life. There are times when he is asked about the future of the world, and he says, in effect, "I don't know." There are times when he is found studying and learning and debating with teachers in the temple. There are even modern theories that Jesus potentially traveled as a youth, learning spiritual wisdom from teachers and sages around the Ancient Near

East—whether this is factual is irrelevant. The truth is that we know Jesus grew in knowledge and spiritual wisdom, and that it took time, energy, and practice, which means that if we want to grow in spiritual wisdom and knowledge, it will require us to take time and discipline to practice and learn as well. Spiritual maturity doesn't happen automatically.

In the same way you can't just walk up to a piano and play Bach, the same is true with spirituality. If you want to grow in spiritual depth, then you must work at it. You must be persistent. You must be disciplined. Even in his thirties, the Gospels tell us that Jesus regularly took time to pray and meditate. He continued to work on his spiritual well-being, even when it was clear that he had grown into a mature spiritual teacher.

What does that say about us? Especially in moments like this, it's easy to let the anxiety and craziness of a crisis pull us away from what is most important. Friend, your spiritual health is important, and I urge you to make time for prayer, meditation, and reflection of Scripture. We, like Jesus, need to ensure that we are growing deeper in our mental and spiritual capacities, especially during difficult seasons of life.

The next aspect of Jesus's humanity that we see in the Scriptures is that Jesus experienced and embraced his emotions. Therefore, we should too. I don't know about you, but so much of the kind of Christianity I found myself within early in my spiritual journey was anti-emotion. I was told that emotions were deceptive and never to be relied upon. I even remember one time sitting in a packed church when I was probably twelve years old, attending the funeral of an eight-year-old boy who'd died in a car accident. I was weeping when my youth pastor came up and said, "You've got to stop crying. If you want to be a pastor, you can't cry." The message was clear: the more spiritual you are, the less emotion you have.

But Jesus shows us exactly the opposite. The shortest verse in all of the Bible is John 11:35, where it simply says, "Jesus wept." This verse follows Jesus receiving the news that his dear friend

Lazarus has died. In the middle of teaching his disciples, Jesus stops, breaks down, and cries. He weeps. He is overcome with sadness and grief at the loss of a loved one. If Jesus, who is the very representation of God, could break down and weep, what does that say about our emotions? If Jesus could feel deep sorrow and grief, what does that say about how we express these intense emotions? I want to suggest that it means that our emotions are sacred. Our feelings reflect the image of God. The fact that we have emotions means that God has emotions. That Jesus felt deeply means that the most human thing we can do is to *feel*.

In this season of our collective human story, it is important that we are taking time to feel, fully. It's easy to want to numb ourselves and zone out, but it is important that we express our feelings. If you're sad, allow yourself to be sad. If you are angry, be angry. If you are deeply disillusioned, express that. Emotions have a way of letting us know what's happening beneath the surface even if we are not fully cognizant of it.

Jesus did not only experience sadness, he experienced the whole range of human emotion, including anger. In Matthew 21:18–21 we have the story of Jesus walking with his disciples and he is clearly quite hungry, but all of the trees around him are barren. So Jesus lashes out and curses the tree—he gets frustrated. He gets hangry! (the anger that emerges when we're overly hungry!) We also have stories of Jesus filled with joy and with anxiety in the Gospel accounts. In all of it, we see Jesus feeling deeply, which should be a signal to all of us that we too should allow ourselves to feel. Your emotions are a gift and are meant to be expressed. To do so makes you not only truly human, but it makes you more like Jesus.

The fourth aspect that Jesus, the human, reveals to us is controversial. I believe it's clearly evidenced in the Gospels: even Jesus made mistakes. Therefore, it's okay for us to make mistakes. Now, of course, the orthodox Christian tradition tells us that Jesus didn't commit any sins. However, there is an older and broader tradition that teaches that part of Jesus growing up into his call-

ing and identity as the Son of God was making mistakes—just
read one of the "infancy gospels" that have young Jesus killing
people in anger, then raising them from the dead. Early Christians
read these texts and seemed to accept the idea of Jesus learning through mistakes. There is one Gospel story that shows Jesus
clearly making a mistake, and then correcting it. It is found in
Matthew 15:22–28:

> A Canaanite woman came to Jesus, crying out, "Lord,
> Son of David, have mercy on me! My daughter is demon-
> possessed and suffering terribly." Jesus did not answer a
> word. So his disciples came to him and urged him, "Send
> her away, for she keeps crying out after us." He answered,
> "I was sent only to the lost sheep of Israel." The woman
> came and knelt before him. "Lord, help me!" she said. He
> replied, "It is not right to take the children's bread and
> toss it to the dogs." "Yes it is, Lord," she said. "Even the
> dogs eat the crumbs that fall from their master's table."
> Then Jesus said to her, "Woman, you have great faith!
> Your request is granted." And her daughter was healed
> at that moment.

This story is deeply troubling. Lots of theologians and scholars have tried to twist it to make it not reveal what it quite clearly
reveals. The breakdown of this story is this: Jesus is walking and
a woman of another ethnic and religious group approaches him,
begging him to heal her daughter, and he completely ignores her,
passes by, doesn't even acknowledge her existence. She keeps following, begging for help. His disciples even urge him to tell her to
go away. He turns around and says, "I have only come to help *my
people*" and keeps walking. She follows, crying, begging for help.
He turns around again and says, "It is not right for me to help
dogs like you." That's right: he utters a slur, calling this woman a
dog, and keeps walking. She yells, "Even dogs deserve crumbs!",
and something in Jesus shifts. He turns around and says, "Woman,

your faith, demonstrated by your persistence, is great. So I will heal your daughter," and he finally heals this woman's daughter.

Now you could interpret this as Jesus simply trying to test a woman's faith. You could interpret this as Jesus simply following the Jewish religious law, which forbade him from interacting with foreigners. Or, you could interpret it in the way that I believe is most apparent—Jesus made a judgment based on ethnic and religious stereotype, but eventually was convicted of this behavior and changed his mind.

One commentator, William O'Brien, says the following, specifically commenting on the woman's response to Jesus that "even dogs deserve scraps":

> Is she debasing herself to save her daughter? Or is she slyly challenging the Rabbi's own blind spot, arguing that God's liberation is not limited by ethnic boundaries? Is she shaming Jesus by confronting him with his own radical theology of "the least of these"? Jesus himself seems startled by her answer. He affirms her wisdom and faith, and, in typical fashion for Mark, implies that her bold spirit played a role in accomplishing her daughter's healing. I am drawn to the radical interpretation that this is a moment when Jesus himself is challenged, in the way he challenges others, to expand his sense of God's reign and God's action. The challenge comes from the margins, from someone on the other side of the divide between the clean and the unclean. I wonder if, in a sense, this encounter is a two-way exorcism: the Syrophoenician woman's daughter is freed from her unclean spirit, and an unclean spirit of residual ethnic chauvinism is cast out of Jesus.[4]

Again, if being orthodox is our highest aim, then this interpretation can't stand. But if we really want to look at Jesus in all his humanity, then I agree with William O'Brien: This is a moment where Jesus messes up, is challenged, and grows. And if that is true, it gives a lot of hope to you and me. Because we all will make mistakes. But Jesus shows us that, even in the parts of us that are most broken, where we have deeply engrained ideologies—like those of racism, sexism, judgment of others—we can change. We can repent, change course, and follow the right path.

Jesus struggled at first to be compassionate to this woman, probably because she was a woman and of another religious sect and ethnicity. But as she challenged him—as she held the mirror of his own teachings up to him—he was convicted of his behavior, turned, and extended healing to her daughter. He ultimately ends up affirming the dignity of this woman, which flew in the face of all the cultural and religious customs of his day, and, in so doing, expanded the reach of God's Kingdom.

If Jesus can learn from his mistakes and can embrace those who challenge him on his blind spots, so can we. So should we. Being freed to see Jesus in the fullness of his humanity like this makes me feel more hopeful that even I can overcome my areas of blindness and prejudice. It reveals the beauty of grace—that it not only covers our flaws and failures, but it enables us to learn, grow, and make right where we've been wrong. Jesus's humanity reveals this in a profound and beautiful way. When we get a glimpse of his full humanity, when we see him as a person just like us, then I believe God's intention in the incarnation is revealed. God became a human to show us it's possible to become the people that we are meant to be.

Jesus shows us that we can live a better life. We *can* be more disciplined and grow more deeply into mature, healthy human beings. Righteousness—which simply means right living—is possible for us all.

5

Love Kindness

Whenever I say the word "kindness," honestly, I feel kind of cheesy. To implore someone to "Be kind" is such a basic, almost childish thing to say. After all, this should be one of the lessons we learn at the earliest stages of our lives. In preschool, we're taught to consider others' feelings and do our best to make people feel good instead of bad. And yet, as basic a value as kindness is, we all struggle with it. And the more that unkindness flourishes in our society, the more we're all drawn deeper into a collective pattern of unkindness.

This is especially true in our social media era—it has become too easy for us to throw out the pursuit of kindness to put out a zinger of a Tweet or Facebook comment that really trashes another person. Think about it—haven't you tweeted or posted or texted something, probably recently, that you would never have said to that person *in person*? But because all that we see is a photo or avatar on a screen, we embrace a kind of amnesia and forget that there is a real person, with real feelings and a real life on the other side of the screen.

People are constantly taking shots at one another on social media. For me, I am tempted to engage in a social media feud at least once a week, if not more. But unkindness is not relegated to the internet—it seems to be growing in our in-person interactions too. We have all seen an unusually rude person in a restaurant.

We all have the obnoxious co-worker who grates on our nerves. We've all been in that meeting where we've said something critical of a colleague to make ourselves look smarter. Kindness is in short supply these days—in others, and if we're honest, within ourselves.

I can't tell you how many times I have written something in the heat of a moment, and then looked back a few days later and have been utterly ashamed of what I said. I can't tell you how many times it's been far easier for me to trash talk someone behind their back than to build them up and speak kindly of them. I struggle with being kind, and I have a feeling I am not alone.

What is even worse is this: If you ask most people of the street what they think about Christians in this day and age, I guarantee you most of them will *not* say we are kind. In fact, they are more likely to say the opposite. Christians—on the left and the right—seem to be some of the unkindest people out there.

On the left, we have cancel culture. If you don't align with our set of social beliefs and political opinions, or you say something that goes against consensus opinion, you're attacked and "canceled"—meaning you're deemed fundamentally ignorant and irrelevant to the conversation. On the right, there is a type of virtual mob that is sent to relentlessly mock and ridicule anyone who doesn't align with "orthodox" political perspectives or religious beliefs. I agree with British journalist Kathrine Whitehorn: "Why do born again people make you often wish they'd never been born the first time?" Christians are some of the most unkind people out there, and that's a shame. But even though I think we are in the midst of an epidemic of unkindness today, we are not the first people to wrestle with this.

One of my favorites among the Hebrew prophets, Micah, talks about it in the context of ancient Israel. As you read through Micah's entire book, you will hear account after account of the people of Israel acting in unjust and unkind ways toward each other. In Micah 2, we read,

How terrible it will be for people who plan wickedness,
who lie on their beds and make evil plans. When the
morning light comes, they do what they planned, because
they have the power to do so. They want fields, so they
take them; they want houses, so they take them away.
They cheat people to get their houses; they rob them even
of their property.

He's describing some pretty evil actions of people. It feels a little
inappropriate to simply call these actions unkind—though they
certainly are—because they far surpass mere unkindness into
being downright evil.

What I want to suggest to you is that unkindness is the first
step down the slippery slope toward injustice. If we begin by
adopting an attitude that enables us to see and speak of others
poorly, then it won't be long until we are justifying unkind actions
toward them. Small actions grow toward bigger ones, and then
you see behaviors like those that Micah lists.

Stealing, cheating, and plotting against people—unkindness is
the initial root of all these evil actions. If you can begin by giving
someone side eye, or gossiping about them, or "canceling" someone, it's not long until you'll justify even more wicked behavior
against them. Which is why later in Micah's writings, when he
describes the core things that God desires from us, kindness is at
the very heart of it all. Micah 6:8 says,

He has told you, O mortal, what is good; and what does
the Lord require of you but to do justice, and to love
kindness, and to walk humbly with your God?

According to the Prophet Micah, God desires three things
from us: doing justice, loving kindness, and walking in humility.
At the heart of this list—right in the center—is kindness. If you're
not kind, you will not do justice. If you are not kind, you will not
be humble. If you are not kind, you will not please or honor God.

So, for God, kindness is much more than a childish command. To God, kindness is at the very heart of who God is calling us to be, and when unkindness flourishes, you can be certain that very soon injustice will begin to rear its ugly head.

Just look around our country today. Take a look at our public conversations and how we react to those who think or vote or believe differently than us. We're not doing a very good job living up to God's high calling for us to love kindness, and we are reaping the consequences.

The Hebrew word that's used in Micah 6:8 for kindness is *chesed*. The actual meaning of this word is loyal love and charity between people, one who goes above and beyond what is required of them—it's more than sentimental niceness. It is an attitude that calls us to intentionally choose to bless others, even those who we don't think deserve it. I love that loyalty is a part of this definition; loyalty means unwavering commitment to do something. When Micah says we must "love kindness," he's saying we must have unwavering commitment to an attitude of kindness. In fact, in the Hebrew Bible, God's love toward the nation of Israel is most often described as *chesed* love: kind, loyal, above and beyond what is deserved love.

Even when the Hebrew people mess up, God is kind. Even when they worship false gods, God is kind. Even when they curse God to his face, God is kind. Even when they commit grand acts of injustice, God is kind. And this is the version of kindness that we're being called to embody as Christians. An attitude that chooses the high road even when others do us wrong, or as Michelle Obama said, "When they go low, we go high." *That's* kindness.

I also want to make another important distinction. When we're talking about kindness, we're not talking about being pushovers. We're not talking about not standing up for what's right. We are not saying to simply accept wrong that is done to us. When we are talking about kindness, we are not talking about "niceness." Lots of people are *nice* but they are not *kind*. Lots of people will be pleasant to your face but stab you in the back. Lots of people will sugarcoat their attitude toward you but have no care for you at all—that's niceness. God doesn't call us to be nice.

Barry Corey, the president of Biola University, wrote a book called *Love Kindness* in which he highlights this distinction between niceness and kindness. This is what he says:

> Our increasingly shrill sounds in the public square are not strengthening our witness but weakening it. Bull horns and fist shaking, mustering armies and using war-waging rhetoric are far less effective than the way of kindness, treating those with whom we disagree with charity and civility. That doesn't mean we don't stand courageously for what we deem is right, true, and just. But kindness is not incompatible with courage.
>
> Kindness embodies courage, but courage does not always embody kindness. Too often our centers are firm on conviction, but our edges are also hard in our tactics. This way is characterized by aggression. On the other hand, there is the way of niceness. Whereas aggression has a firm center and hard edges, niceness has soft edges and a spongy center. Niceness may be pleasant, but it lacks conviction. It has no soul.[5]

Dr. Corey highlights three attitudes we can take. First, he highlights the harshness that is so prevalent in our culture today. We will call out anyone, fight with anyone, tear down anyone. We throw out civility in the name of "justice" and that only hurts our witness as followers of Jesus. People see us as harsh and rude and don't want to engage with us. We may have firm convictions, but our edges are sharp and leave a lot of people with wounds.

Then there is niceness. Nice people refuse to take a stand on any issue. It's soft and comfortable, but as Dr. Corey says, it has no soul. It doesn't stand for what is right; it stands for nothing. It looks good on the outside but is empty on the inside.

Most of us will lean toward one or the other of these postures. Some of us are harsh: loving conflict, loving arguing, and going right in and speaking up and calling people out. Some of us are nice: hating conflict, so we won't say anything offensive or hurtful, but inside, thinking all sorts of judgmental things and growing resentful that nothing ever changes. Neither harshness nor niceness gets us where we want to go. If you are harsh, people won't listen to you and will most often be more solidified in their opposition of you. If you are nice, no one will rely on you or care what you have to say, because it has no real substance.

But kindness is firm on the inside and soft on the outside. It considers people's feelings and emotions. It truly wants the best for everyone involved. It's willing to sacrifice itself for the good of others, while also drawing lines and standing firm. It's willing to speak with clarity and civility. It refuses to attack the dignity and value of individuals but will certainly critique their ideas or behaviors that are wrong. Kindness allows for spirited disagreement while still honoring and respecting one another as humans.

You can begin to see why kindness is such a core value in Micah's teaching. Without kindness, we're on a slippery slope toward all manner of injustice. You see, to begin the process of demonizing someone, you must first begin by dehumanizing them. Once we fail to see that another person is a human being, we can begin to treat them less than kindly. Eventually, we will strip them so completely of their human dignity that we can do all manner of atrocities to them. When we allow ourselves to treat others as disembodied ideologies, as less than humans made in God's image, we are beginning the dehumanizing process. And in dehumanizing them, we are denigrating the very image and glory of God within them.

One of the most foundational beliefs of both the Jewish and Christian tradition is that every human is made in the image and likeness of God. That means we believe that if you want to see what God is like, you simply have to look into the face of your neighbor. Even the neighbor who is a Trump supporter. Even the neighbor who is pro-choice. Even the neighbor whose dog consistently makes a mess in your yard. Even the neighbor who makes you uncomfortable by the way they dress. God's image is present in each one of these people. God's life and light is present in each one of them. When you begin to walk with your eyes wide open to *that* reality, you set yourself on the path to embodying kindness.

Throughout his book, Micah points out the many sins that the people of Israel have committed that provoked the anger of God, so much so that God pours out judgment on them. But even amid the anger and judgment, God continued to respond with kindness. There was always a path toward reconciliation, restoration, and redemption. Despite their lack of deserving, from a human perspective, God's kindness, God extended it to them. We are called to embody that same kind of posture toward one another. When we acknowledge God's image in one another, we are walking in the path of kindness.

Kindness is also the only effective path to bring about true change in our world. As followers of Jesus, we are walking in the footsteps of a man who quite literally incarnated kindness. Jesus, even confronted with people who hated him so much they wanted to kill him, embodied kindness. Not because he was weak, but because he was strong, and because he knew that if you want to change this world—to change the hearts and minds of people and inspire them to live in a new way—you have to do it with kindness.

Critique does not change lives. Criticism doesn't change minds. Arguing and lambasting someone will not help them see differently. It is *kindness* that unlocks the potential for transformation. The Bible says it is the kindness of God that leads us to repentance (Romans 2:4). Not wrath. Not condemnation. No, it is grace that saves us. It is kindness that changes us. And if that's true on a cosmic level, it is certainly true on a political level. It is certainly true in your workplace. It's certainly true in your relationships. Kindness brings about transformation. Civility brings about openness. If you want to change the world, you have to do it by being kind.

Through kindness, gentleness, and openness, we can open the door to changing each other's minds. To changing ourselves. Again, kindness is what leads us to repentance. Repentance literally means "to expand one's mind" or "change one's course." If you want to bring about change in your workplace, in your family, with your kids, or in this nation, we won't do it through polarizing rhetoric, harsh judgment, or constant critique. We'll do it through being kind. Through speaking truth but covered with grace. Through treating the other as if they bear the very image of God, while also calling them toward the way of justice and truth. Kindness isn't a call to inaction or complacency—it is exactly the opposite. Have your political convictions—we must!—but for God's sake be kind about it. Have your religious conversations—they're important—but be kind about it. Tell your spouse the things that they're doing that's putting strain on the relationship, but do it drenched in kindness.

You see, kindness is anything but a childish virtue. It's a high calling, incredibly hard, and just may be the thing that can actually change our world. Friends, there is but one human family, one people made in the image of one God. We all have different experiences that lead us to have different views, and all our experiences are valid. When we relate to one another with an attitude of kindness, things in our world will begin to change. More than that, we will be honoring the heart of God's requirement for us. What does the Lord require of you, the Prophet Micah rhetorically asks: that you do justice, love kindness, and walk humbly with your God?

6

Playing Favorites

I was never a very popular kid in school. Not only was I shy, not only did I have a high-pitched soprano voice until late in my high school years, not only was I unathletic, not only was I the weird closeted gay Christian boy who told everyone they were going to hell unless they joined my church, but I also had a horrendous bowl cut: I think *that* was the primary reason I was never really popular in school.

Another reason I know why I was excluded often growing up was because I lived in one of the wealthiest zip codes in the nation, just a half hour drive outside of Washington, DC. Most of my peers had wealthy and powerful parents who lived in massive homes, went on lavish vacations, could afford the most stylish clothes. I, on the other hand, grew up in a trailer park with a family who struggle to pay our bills let alone go on vacation to five-star resorts.

I remember one memory, when I was sitting in the cafeteria at lunch and a group of boys started taunting me for living in a "tin can"—my mobile home's siding was made of sheets of tin, and apparently, that was a sign of a cheaper home. So, they kept jeering: "Brandan, you live in a tin can." And me, being the kid who tried to hide my family's financial situation, who tried so hard to blend in with my wealthy friends, felt deeply ashamed. My friends laughed and scoffed at me, and I felt less-than for something that I couldn't control.

Have you ever had an experience like this? Have you ever been on the receiving end of discrimination—of others playing favorites—and been really hurt by it? I can't claim to know discrimination as many other minorities have in our country, but I've had my fair share of humiliation and pain.

Have you ever seen someone, maybe for the first time, and just automatically known that you didn't like them? Like you had some sort of inner sense of repulsion or emotional judgment that immediately tinted your lens and you automatically pushed them away? I do this far too often. I judge people without knowing them. I judge them based on external and artificial standards. And can I just also admit that a lot of the time the people I judge as worth my time and attention based on those same external standards are actually pretty terrible people?

This issue of judging people, of playing favorites, is exactly what the Apostle James spills a great deal of ink addressing in chapter 2 of his epistle:

> My dear friends, don't let public opinion influence how you live out our glorious, Christ-originated faith. If a man enters your church wearing an expensive suit, and a street person wearing rags comes in right after him, and you say to the man in the suit, "Sit here, sir; this is the best seat in the house!" and either ignore the street person or say, "Better sit here in the back row," haven't you segregated God's children and proved that you are judges who can't be trusted?
>
> Listen, dear friends. Isn't it clear by now that God operates quite differently? He chose the world's down-and-out as the kingdom's first citizens, with full rights and privileges. This kingdom is promised to anyone who loves God. And here you are abusing these same citizens! Isn't it the high and mighty who exploit you, who use the courts to rob you blind? Aren't they the ones who scorn the new name—"Christian"—used in your baptisms?

You do well when you complete the Royal Rule of the Scriptures: "Love others as you love yourself." But if you play up to these so-called important people, you go against the Rule and stand convicted by it. You can't pick and choose in these things, specializing in keeping one or two things in God's law and ignoring others. The same God who said, "Don't commit adultery," also said, "Don't murder." If you don't commit adultery but go ahead and murder, do you think your non-adultery will cancel out your murder? No, you're a murderer, period.

Talk and act like a person expecting to be judged by the Rule that sets us free. For if you refuse to act kindly, you can hardly expect to be treated kindly. Kind mercy wins over harsh judgment every time. (MSG)

It seems to me that there are three timeless lessons that James is trying to communicate about how we, as followers of his elder brother, Jesus, are to conduct ourselves not only within the church but in our day-to-day lives.

The first thing is this: don't judge other people based on cultural standards and external appearances. Again, what's refreshing about James's letter is that the same problems we deal with today are the problems that humans were dealing with about two thousand years ago when he wrote this. Not much has changed. He gives us a potent example: what if someone walks into worship dressed in a three-piece suit or a remarkably stunning dress and sits next to you? Most of us would probably either be delighted and want to introduce ourselves, or at least not mind that they were sitting next to us. But then consider what would happen if the opposite happened, and one of your homeless neighbors enters wearing tattered and dirty clothes and sits next to you. How would you respond? Or, perhaps a timelier example. What if someone walks in wearing a political t-shirt supporting the political candidate who is completely opposed to what you stand for in every way, and moves to sit down next to you? How would you respond?

Most of us might be kind and courteous in both cases, but our external actions are not really the problem. Sure, it's great that most of us would try to be respectful, but what is happening on the inside? What are you thinking? What kind of judgments are you making? Are you assuming that the wealthy person must have their lives together? That they must be a good person? And are you assuming that the person with tattered clothes has made bad choices? Or is potentially a threat to you?

What about the person who comes in representing a party or candidate other than yours? Are you assuming they're an idiot, uneducated, or stuck up? What *are* you thinking? The first question we need to ask ourselves is, why? Why are we so quick to make judgments about others? Especially when we know that people's lives and stories are far more complex than their outward appearance might suggest. Then, the deeper question we should be asking is, Does our mind-set reflect God's? Doesn't it make sense to believe God's truth about people before we believe our own preconceived judgments or ideas about someone? And what is God's mind-set?

James writes,

> Isn't it clear by now that God operates quite differently? He chose the world's down-and-out as the kingdom's first citizens, with full rights and privileges. This kingdom is promised to anyone who loves God. And here you are abusing these same citizens!

In this Scripture is a really beautiful truth: the church is first and foremost for those who are considered "the world's down-and-out," those who may not seem wise or of high esteem by the world's standards. This community is for those who have made mistakes, who are far less than perfect, who continue to make mistakes, and continue to struggle. This community is a place where we are called to suspend judgment and suspend all of our external identities. The amount of money in your bank account doesn't matter in the Body of Christ. Who you love doesn't matter here. Where you live doesn't matter here.

Not that these aspects of our identities aren't important—of course they are. They create the circumstances of our lives. But the fundamental truth is that each person is made in the image and likeness of God, each human is a child of God, and because of that common identity, we are all absolutely equal. The playing field is leveled. We are told that God's love is extended, first and foremost, to those who are rough around the edges, and yet how often do we act in a completely opposite way? We favor those who, by external appearance, seem to be what our culture deems as "important" or "put together."

Therefore, James says, "Don't let public opinion influence how you live out our glorious, Christ-originated faith." What our culture deems valuable is usually, upon deeper reflection, the least valuable aspect of a person. The clothes you wear, the money you have, the opinions you hold, the job you work, are ultimately not important. You can lose any of those things in a moment—and yet you are still, forever, a beloved child of God with purpose and immeasurable value.

The problem is that most of us don't believe this about ourselves, and if we don't believe it for ourselves, we'll have a really hard time believing it about others. In this moment of history, our self-doubt and self-hatred is at an ultimate high. We see images every day of people who are hotter than we are, wealthier than we are, have done more than we have done, who travel more, who have a healthier family, a better partner, who seem to be more joyful than we are. We interpret their apparent joy and well-being as a judgment on who we fundamentally are: We are less than. We are broken. We are not good enough. Our lives are meaningless.

Many of us have this record of self-doubt playing on repeat in our heads, and when we begin to believe these things about ourselves, we also begin to project them on others. We begin to compare ourselves to those who, by our assessment are "less than us," and we treat these people as less valuable. But it is all a lie, an illusion. The things we think that are most important about people are not the most important at all.

The Scriptures teach us that everyone should be treated with dignity and respect in our life. Everyone should have a chance to prove themselves to us. By projecting our own self-hatred on to others, we not only harm other people who can feel our judgment, but we prevent ourselves from getting to know amazing people who more often than not can be bigger blessings to us than we ever could have imagined.

One of my best friends is a guy who I first looked at from across a room and made a snap judgment about. At first glance, I deduced that he was a stuck-up, privileged individual who thought he was too good to talk to me. I projected my own negative self-image onto him, and began actively disliking him. Then one day when we were at a bar with mutual friends, we started talking. In just a few moments, I discovered that he was an incredibly genuine person, who cared for others in such a deep way. I had projected my own pain and lack of confidence onto him, and if it wasn't for an unlikely conversation, I would have missed out on a great friend.

I know another person who has far less than I have, who struggles with health and with finances. When I first saw him, my natural impulse was to turn the other way, to not acknowledge him, and avoid being uncomfortable hearing about his situation that seemed so different from mine. And then, I got to know him. He *does* have a lot of struggles and quirks, but he is also one of the funniest, smartest people I know. My judgment could have kept me from getting to know him, just because he didn't look like what I've been conditioned to believe is "normal."

How many people in your life have you prematurely judged and missed out on a relationship with? And how many people have we robbed of their dignity by treating them in a disrespectful, impatient, or judgmental way? How many people do you walk by every day on the street, who are real human beings with stories and feelings and needs and hopes, yet we do everything in our power not to make eye contact, to treat them as if they didn't exist, as if they weren't human beings? We have a crisis in our culture of unseen people. A crisis of people who surround us every day, who yearn for a loving glance, a kind word, a person to talk to, but because of something external and artificial, we ignore them, we rob them of their God-given value, and treat them as less than human.

According to Scripture, you are valuable. You deserve love. You deserve friendship. You deserve to know that *nothing is fundamentally wrong with you*, and that your circumstances and situation do not define you. This is the truth, and it is the heart of the Gospel, and to those of us who fail to express due dignity and love to others, we've got to make a change. We've got to work to overcome our judgmental attitudes and see past the external circumstances of people—see their value and beauty as our siblings in God.

Which brings me to the second point James teaches: To fulfill the law of God is to love one another and to love ourselves. According to James and Jesus, if we want to fulfill all of God's laws and requirements, this is the only and highest requirement: to treat everyone with love and respect. James writes,

> You do well when you complete the Royal Rule of the Scriptures: "Love others as you love yourself." But if you play up to these so-called important people, you go against the Rule and stand convicted by it. You can't pick and choose in these things, specializing in keeping one or two things in God's law and ignoring others. The same God who said, "Don't commit adultery," also said, "Don't murder." If you don't commit adultery but go ahead and murder, do you think your non-adultery will cancel out your murder? No, you're a murderer, period.
>
> Talk and act like a person expecting to be judged by the Rule that sets us free. For if you refuse to act kindly, you can hardly expect to be treated kindly. Kind mercy wins over harsh judgment every time.

James says that the "Royal Rule of Scripture" is to love others as you love yourself. He says that when we respect people based on their status or appearance or wealth, we are failing to follow God's most basic and yet highest law. Then, as he warns us not to judge others, he says,

> Talk and act like a person expecting to be judged by the Rule that sets us free. For if you refuse to act kindly, you can hardly expect to be treated kindly. Kind mercy wins over harsh judgment every time.

Don't judge. Short and sweet. Notice that he doesn't say, *If you judge, God's going to judge you.* That's how toxic religion teaches people about God. The God revealed in Jesus is a God of redemption, who is willing to forgive us when we screw up, and willing to help restore, redirect, and guide us toward healing, wholeness, and a better life. But James *does* say that if we live as judgmental people, we're going to be judged by the law of love, and by other people. This principle of reciprocity is at the heart of so much of Scripture. If you sow judgment, you will reap it. If you treat others poorly, you will be treated poorly. If you love and respect yourself, you will be loved and respected by others.

The other side of this judgment is this: if we are building our lives around the example of Jesus, we will gradually see our mind-set changing to be more Christlike, and when we act in ways that are contrary to the way of Jesus—judging others, favoring others—we will feel the Spirit's conviction. Conviction is a good thing—to feel guilt when we do something wrong, that's a gift from God, a human impulse that calls us deeper into a path of health and wholeness. And when we practice the law of love, when we work to rewire our way of thinking so that we stop automatically judging ourselves or others we will be set free from these toxic patterns.

This is true freedom: to be able to see others for who they are—beloved children of God, equal to us. The ability to love ourselves, to see ourselves as children of God, and not to live in the trap of the cycle of comparison. Following the law of love is what sets us free to live the truly abundant life that God desires for each one of us.

7

The Fourth Man in the Fire

If you grew up in the West, you have been shaped by the Bible. Religious or not, whether you have ever picked up a copy of the Bible or not, you have been shaped by the Bible. Its themes and stories shape our culture—from the way we keep time, to the holidays we celebrate, to the cultural metaphors that we use. The Bible and its stories have formed the very foundation of the world that we live in.

If you grew up in an environment that was even nominally Christian, you probably are familiar with the wide array of Bible stories that we tend to teach our children. Stories like Adam and Eve, Noah's Ark, Daniel and the Lion's Den, the Exodus, Jonah and the Whale, David and Goliath, Samson and Delilah. Visit any great art museum and you will be inundated with images associated with these classic tales. We decorate our children's nurseries with cute arks with fuzzy animals. We read versions of these stories to our kids as we put them to sleep at night. We believe they convey good, light-hearted lessons about how we should be brave, have faith in God, and how we can rest in the love of our Creator. But have you ever stopped and reflected on a lot of these innocent stories we tell our children? Have you ever looked them up in the actual text of the Bible and read them? If you have, you will notice a few surprising things about them.

First, most of these stories are not very interesting in the Bible. They tend to be quite short, lacking in details, and there is little real character development in the stories themselves. This can be shocking because the versions of these stories that we tell our children are often filled with colorful images and details.

The other, more pertinent thing you will discover as you read these stories in the Bible is that a lot of them are *really messed up*. They usually cover very adult topics and are very violent or cruel. They also paint an image of God that many of us probably don't believe in—a mythical image of a deity who is vengeful and delights in blood sacrifices, who plays games with human lives, and whose actions don't seem to resemble those of a God of mercy and grace at all.

As rough as these stories are, as strange and shocking as they may be, they are the stories our ancestors have passed down to us. For thousands of years, billions of people have looked at them and found direction, hope, and insight about God and themselves. This is the beautiful tension that exists within the Bible. This tension is what emerges when we decide to engage with the text faithfully but also logically and realistically. I believe that the Spirit that is within you and me also inspired folks to sit down and write out their own stories and experience of God long ago so that we might wrestle with and learn from their perspectives. These humans, like us, have finite perspectives. They're doing their best to describe the world as they see it and God as they understand God. Sometimes they say crazy stuff that we *should* disagree with. Stuff that doesn't align with how we've come to understand God, life, or the world. And that's okay.

One of my favorite Bible stories is the tale of three faithful Jewish men—Shadrach, Meshach, and Abednego—who are forced to choose between obeying God and obeying their king. This story comes from the Book of Daniel, chapter 3. This is what the text says:

> King Nebuchadnezzar made an image of gold, sixty cubits high and six cubits wide, and set it up on the plain of Dura in the province of Babylon. He then summoned

the satraps, prefects, governors, advisers, treasurers,
judges, magistrates and all the other provincial officials
to come to the dedication of the image he had set up.
So the satraps, prefects, governors, advisers, treasurers,
judges, magistrates and all the other provincial officials
assembled for the dedication of the image that King
Nebuchadnezzar had set up, and they stood before it.
(Daniel 3:1–3, NIV)

We're introduced to a king named Nebuchadnezzar, whom
scholars believe is a mythological figure based on the Neo-Babylo-
nian King Nabonidus. Between 556 and 539 BC, Nabonidus took
the throne of the Babylonian Kingdom by force and angered the people of the empire by downgrading the status of the god of Babylon,
Marduk, and elevating his personal god, Sin, the god of the moon.
The story begins with this corrupt king creating a god of gold to be
worshiped by all of the people of the empire, from his highest advisers to the lowest commoner. This is a power move: If the king can
gain control of the religion of the empire, he knows he can control
the people. So, he lowers their beloved god and elevates his own—a
display of the superiority of Sin over Marduk, and of King Nebuchadnezzar over the previous kings of Babylon. The text continues.

Then the herald loudly proclaimed, "Nations and peoples
of every language, this is what you are commanded to do:
As soon as you hear the sound of the horn, flute, zither,
lyre, harp, pipe and all kinds of music, you must fall down
and worship the image of gold that King Nebuchadnezzar
has set up. Whoever does not fall down and worship will
immediately be thrown into a blazing furnace."
Therefore, as soon as they heard the sound of the
horn, flute, zither, lyre, harp and all kinds of music, all
the nations and peoples of every language fell down and
worshiped the image of gold that King Nebuchadnezzar
had set up. (Daniel 3:4–7, NIV)

The herald of the king declares that when the music begins, the king demands that everyone in the empire bow down and worship this new god of the king. Again, in the ancient world, obedience to the king's god was obedience to the king, and in a pagan culture where gods were a dime a dozen, being made to worship a new deity would have been frustrating to the citizens of Babylon but would not be seen as a huge moral or religious issue. They would have likely worshiped the god Sin already, just as a lesser god to their supreme deity. So, they understood, by and large, that this was just a symbolic acknowledgment that a new king was in town and that the people of Babylon were submitting to this new king's power and authority. The text continues:

> At this time some astrologers came forward and denounced the Jews. They said to King Nebuchadnezzar, "May the king live forever! Your Majesty has issued a decree that everyone who hears the sound of the horn, flute, zither, lyre, harp, pipe and all kinds of music must fall down and worship the image of gold, and that whoever does not fall down and worship will be thrown into a blazing furnace. But there are some Jews whom you have set over the affairs of the province of Babylon—Shadrach, Meshach and Abednego—who pay no attention to you, Your Majesty. They neither serve your gods nor worship the image of gold you have set up." (Daniel 3:8–12, NIV)

The word "astrologers" is in fact better translated *Chaldeans*, which is another name for the Babylonian people. Some of the Babylonians who had submitted to the king's new authority had noticed that some of the Jews whom the king had appointed to high levels in the province were refusing to obey the king's command, and by refusing to bow before the idol the king set up, they were symbolically saying, "We do not accept your authority as our king." But there is also something shadier happening here— these Babylonians seem jealous. They are native to the land, and the Jews living in Babylon are there as captives who had been conquered and dominated by the powerful Babylonian Empire. But for some reason, the king has appointed three Jewish men to serve in his administration, not as servants, but as those who direct the king's affairs.

One can imagine that these jealous Babylonians have been waiting for an opportunity to get these men removed from their post. Have you ever experienced jealous people in your life? People who didn't like you for no good reason, and made it their goal to cut you down every time they got the chance? Oftentimes, when we receive blessing or taste success in our lives, there are people standing by who get angry because they think they deserve to be the ones who are elevated or because they think someone like *you* definitely should not. These people are poisoned with bitterness, usually stemming from a selfish, ego-centered mindset that leads them to believe they are fundamentally better than others and therefore deserving of status, position, or promotion. They can't seem to stand it when other people, whom they deem less worthy, get elevated before them.

That is what these Babylonian tattletales are doing. They are racist: they see the Jewish people as less than and can't stand that three Jewish men have received such status within the king's administration. So, they run to tell the king of their disobedience as soon as they get the chance. The text continues by describing King Nebuchadnezzar's rage when he discovers that Shadrach, Meshach, and Abednego wouldn't bow down to his gods. He gives an ultimatum: either they bow, right now before his gods, or they will be thrown into a blazing furnace and killed. Of course, the three men stand firm in their faith. They respond declaring that their God will protect them from his persecution, but then they say something profound and peculiar:

> But even if he does not [deliver us], we want you to know,
> Your Majesty, that we will not serve your gods or worship
> the image of gold you have set up. (Daniel 3:18, NIV)

This boldness is incredible. These men are summoned before the king who demands that they bow down to this image in front of him, but Shadrach, Meshach, and Abednego stand bravely and declare that "*we do not need to defend ourselves before you in this matter.*" How many of us know that, when we know that we're confident that we're doing the right thing, we can have the attitude of "I don't need to defend myself"?

This reminds me of the laws in San Diego, where I once lived, which made it illegal to give food in public to people experiencing homelessness. You could literally be fined or arrested in San Diego County for giving food to someone in need. There are all sorts of justifications given for this by public officials, but the truth is that there is nothing wrong with feeding the hungry. In fact, it is a mandate of our faith. So, every single week, members of our church community were willingly going out and handing out food to those in need in violation of the city's law. Was it a risk? It was. Could there have been consequences? There sure could have been. But their attitude was the same as Shadrach, Meshach, and Abednego: "We do not have to defend ourselves in this matter." Because everyone knows, deep within ourselves, that giving what we have to bless others is the right thing to do, even if the government says it is wrong.

Our faith has a long tradition of those refusing to obey laws that call them out of alignment with the values of the faith. We must do what is right, because our ultimate allegiance is to God, not to public officials.

Christianity has a long tradition of civil disobedience. Throughout our two-thousand-year history, we have a strong track record of willfully disobeying the laws of the land that seek to force us to do something out of alignment with the way of Jesus, and we have often paid a great price for such acts of resistance. But the question that we are forced to grapple with when faced with a situation like the one Shadrach, Meshach, and Abednego find themselves in is this: do we really believe what we say we believe?

If we really do believe that Jesus was right when he told us to feed the poor—then how could we allow ourselves to obey a law that calls us to do something different? If the abolitionists really believed that every human being of every race and culture was made in the image of God, how could they comply with the laws of their lands that said that people of African descent were less than fully human? If we really believe that Jesus is Lord, and if we really have committed our lives to following his example and leaning on his Spirit, then we must resist anyone who calls us to contradict what we know is right and good in the eyes of God.

This is precisely what Shadrach, Meshach, and Abednego are doing. They are serving the king well and have proven that they are good workers. Clearly, they have shown the king that they are *so good* that he appointed them despite their being Jewish. And now, when the king is on an ego trip and demanding that everyone worship his god as a display of loyalty to himself, Shadrach, Meshach, and Abednego stand firm on their convictions. The Torah forbids faithful Jews from worshiping a graven image. This is one of the commandments that Moses received directly from God in the Ten Commandments. So, while Shadrach, Meshach, and Abednego were faithful servants of the king, their ultimate allegiance was to their God above everything else. They held their personal values—what they knew was right—to be more important than favorable standing with King Nebuchadnezzar, and so they resist. They say, "We will not bow down. We will obey God. And will we trust that God will deliver us for doing what is right."

That's real faith, isn't it? The ability to stand firm, believing that God will protect you so long as you stay faithful and true to what's right. The ability to face the most powerful political leader in your world and say, "What you're asking me to do is wrong, and I will not obey. Let the consequences come, but I will trust in God." Such faith was rare in their day, and it's rare in ours. Oh, that Christians would be a people who would stand up to the powers that be and declare that our allegiance to doing what is right is more important to us that receiving the favor of the king!

But what I find so profound about this story is that Shadrach, Meshach, and Abednego don't end with just a declaration of faith—they say something even more radical. They say, "We're trusting God to deliver us. *But even if he doesn't,* we still will stand and do what is right." They had an "even if" faith—the ability to stand and do what is right, regardless of whether God was going to deliver them from the consequences of their civil disobedience. This "even if" faith is remarkable. Do you have an "even if" faith? A faith that trusts in God even if things don't go your way? A faith that believes that there is a purpose for your lives and the world, even when everything falls apart?

The "even if" faith of Shadrach, Meshach, and Abednego is the kind of faith that God is looking for in us. Are you a Christian because you want stuff from God? I have often heard people say, "I am losing faith because I've prayed and nothing happened." Or, "My life isn't what I dreamed it would be. Why doesn't God care?" While I understand the doubt and disappointment, the God revealed in Jesus is a God who desires to do good for you by leading you onto the right path of living—not through Divine magic. The path of simple living, generosity, of peace. Jesus taught that the path toward abundant life was one marked by sacrifice. That is where the abundant life springs from. Nothing else will give you abundance of purpose. Nothing else will heal your deepest wounds.

What we should be working toward is an "even if" faith. A faith committed to following Jesus, even when it doesn't benefit us. A faith steadfast in God's goodness and wisdom, even when our own mind tells us to act in a different way. We need an "even if" faith that allows us to stand for what is right regardless of the circumstances, regardless of what's in it for us. This is the faith of Shadrach, Meshach, and Abednego. They knew what was right and they clung to hope that God could deliver them. They clung to the truth that God's ways are better than the human way.

The story concludes with the king heating the furnace hotter than it ever had been heated and having Shadrach, Meshach, and Abednego thrown into the fire. The text tells us that the king watches with great delight until he immediately notices that there are not three men in the fire, but four, and they are walking about the flames unscathed. Immediately, he has the furnace opened and calls for the men to come out of the flames, and when they do, the king finds that not a hair on their head had been burnt by the flames. Shadrach, Meshach, and Abednego proclaim that God was with them in the fire and protected them because of their faithfulness. Seeing this, the king relents of his defiance to the God of Shadrach, Meshach, and Abednego, and instead, restores them to their high-level positions in his government.

Their resistance to a corrupt leader leads them into a dire situation—they are to be bound up and murdered for standing up to the king. But even in their impending death, these men stand firm in their faith in God and their values. I don't know if you've experienced this, but it is often in dire moments, at the very last second, that God seems to do their best work. Shadrach, Meshach, and Abednego are cast into the fire, and immediately "one like son of God" appears and protects them. Notice that the writers go a great length to communicate that this furnace wasn't survivable; the guards who threw the men in the fire died because the heat was so strong. There was literally no hope in this circumstance from a human perspective. But from a faith perspective, Shadrach, Meshach, and Abednego called out to God, trusting that their faithfulness would be met with God's protection. And God does indeed protect them in the midst of the flames.

In this impossible circumstance, their faith is rewarded by God showing up and protecting them. Shadrach, Meshach, and Abednego didn't demand God to show up. They hoped for it. But even if he didn't, they committed to be faithful. That kind of powerful, resistant faith is what seems to move the heart of God. A faith that does not demand but remains open. That kind of faith is fertile soil for miracles. The kind of faith that stands up to the powerful and the mighty. The kind of faith that chooses to do what is right, even if it is hard or costly. The kind of faith that follows Jesus even when no one else is around. That's the kind of faith that can sustain you during dire circumstances, when the flames of hell surround you.

Another lesson from this story is that faithful resistance *works*. We come from a long tradition of people who, on the basis of their faith and commitment to God, stand up against injustice in the highest places of society, who refuse to be silent or to quietly comply with laws or regulations that contradict what we know to be right. A people who are willing to resist in order to shine a light on injustice. That kind of faithful resistance is blessed and protected by God. In the midst of that faith resistance, when the fire gets hotter and hotter, God stands with us. God is in our midst. And even the hearts of kings, mayors, councilmembers, presidents, bosses, parents, and pastors can be changed in an instant through the power of faithful resistance. Through the power of "even if" faith.

Why do we believe in God? Why do we follow Jesus? Is it because we believe that it is right and true? Because we believe it's the path to create a better life and world? Or is it because we want God to give us stuff? Is our faith willing to resist injustice and evil? Are we willing to sacrifice ourselves, our comfort, and our possessions to receive the deeper fulfillment that God promises to those who follow this path?

It is my sincere hope and prayer that Christians—and all people—become a community that embodies the "even if" faith of Shadrach, Meshach, and Abednego. The kind of faith that clings to what is right and good and stands strong in the face of injustice whatever the cost. My faith is not there yet, but I am praying, with God's help, that it will develop and grow within me.

8

Rhythms of Abundance

We are all searching for a life that is full, a life that has meaning, a life of purpose. We are all seeking satisfaction. It's this impulse, unique to humans, that is the genesis of every religious and spiritual path. Since the dawn of human consciousness, we have been longing to make sense of our individual and corporate existence on planet earth. Why are we here? Where are we going? And how do we find fulfillment?

Every one of us has asked these questions. Every one of us has had a sense of dissatisfaction, a vacuum, and a hole within us that we long to fill. The pursuit of filling that void is what many traditions have called the path to salvation, awakening, or enlightenment. And the fact that since the dawn of consciousness, humans have searched for "fulfillment" or that which could fill that void, and every generation continues to ask the questions and seek the path that leads to a full life, suggests that perhaps that which we are seeking is at some level unattainable.

For so many of us, salvation or awakening is thought to be a life of peace, of bliss, of abundance, of light. A life without pain, struggle, or trial. Isn't this at some level what we long for? It is this kind of life that we often project on to our religious gurus—we think they've somehow tapped into a life of true and enduring peace and joy? But when one gets under the surface of their lives, we often find that, in fact, their pursuit for meaning and satisfaction never ended. They too experienced continual longing for something more.

To be human is to be shaped by pain, trials, challenges, and suffering. That is how we grow and mature. That is not to say that we should seek out suffering—I don't want to glorify suffering or longing—but I want to acknowledge that this is fundamentally what it means to be human.

My spiritual guide is Jesus Christ, and a simple scanning of the Gospel accounts of his life will reveal that while we can all agree that Jesus was one of the most awakened beings ever to grace our planet, he too experienced a life of loss, trials, and longing for something more. Yet it is Jesus who tells us that his whole mission in the world is to show us how to have life and life to the fullest. What we can deduce, then, is that an abundant or full life isn't a life free from suffering or longing. Instead, it is a life that makes room for all of these realities while also pursuing meaning, purpose, and wholeness. So, what does it mean to have an abundant life? How do we do it?

As I have studied the life and teachings of Jesus, I have found something that I call "the rhythm of abundance," which is a pattern that we can embrace every day that will result in a more meaningful, fuller life. When we hear the word "abundance" or "abundant life," our culture and society have conditioned us to immediately think of wealth, health, and success. But that's not what it actually means at all. At the heart of our culture's definition of an abundant life is the idea that if we work hard enough, we can be successful, and success looks like wealth, sex, notoriety, and pleasure. Donald Trump is an icon of this "American Dream." The idea that through working hard one can gain unlimited wealth, property, women, and fame. His TV show, *The Apprentice* (and his presidency), was based on this notion—that Trump reflected the American Dream of a fulfilled and satisfied life.

The problem with the American Dream is that it simply does not work. We all know this intuitively, right? We look at celebrities who rise to fame and fortune, who have everything that is supposed to give them a meaningful life, and yet so often, once they're at the top, they give in to addictions and compulsions to help cope with the profound emptiness they feel. They've been lied to and deceived. They have everything they're supposed to have, yet they are just as hollow or empty as ever. Trump himself reflects this. During the election, when Trump's notoriety was skyrocketing and he had never been more famous, wealthy, or powerful, the *New York Times* reported,

> It has been his pride and his palace, a soaring black sky-scraper overlooking Manhattan that seemed to match Donald J. Trump's ambition and ostentatiousness. But Trump Tower, since Friday afternoon, has become a kind of lonely fortress for its most famous occupant, who holes up inside, increasingly isolated and upset, denounced almost every hour by another Republican official. So he remained inside his enormous penthouse apartment on the 66th floor, and his corporate suite 40 stories below, for almost all of Friday and Saturday.[6]

Could it be that at the height of power, fame, and notoriety, Mr. Trump began once again to feel the hollowness of the American Dream, the path to awakening of which he had become the chief guru?

Even our spiritual traditions have adopted these ideas. We have taken deeply true spiritual teachings and laws and tried to exploit them to help us get health, wealth, and prosperity—everything from the wildly popular book, *The Secret*, that promised individuals could manifest anything in their lives through vision casting, to the teaching that if one gives money to their church, God will bless them with upward mobility, healing, and wealth. But we know that the path of consumerist capitalistic success doesn't bring us awakening. This path of "more, more, more" is a dead end.

The other popular path that has emerged throughout the human search for meaning is the path of embracing and exalting suffering and poverty, believing that through leaving behind all of the necessities of human life, and subjecting ourselves to suffering, we can find awakening. This path has always been seen as a noble one, even today. We have great reverence for those who leave everything behind to live a life of great hardship. They seem so profoundly spiritual. And while there is great truth that by giving up our attachment to material possessions, identities, and the hedonistic pursuit of pleasure and success, we can open ourselves to the Divine, when this path becomes exploited as the singular path of awakening, it becomes just as much a dead end and danger as the American Dream. Just read the diaries of the honest monk, Thomas Merton. You will quickly find that being an ascetic is no more helpful to awakening than a seminary degree or great wealth. Merton went to the monastery believing that its asceticism would show him everything, but soon discovered that asceticism wasn't the way.

Both of these paths, the path of more and the pass of less, are by themselves wholly insufficient to lead us to an abundant and full life. But what happens if we were to take them together and create a rhythm, a daily practice and pattern of living? What would happen then?

This is precisely what Jesus demonstrates and calls us to. See, when Jesus talked about abundant life, he called it "The Kingdom of God." Whenever you see those words in the Bible, you can retranslate them in your mind as "the abundant life." Another way I like to say it is this: When Jesus refers to the Kingdom of God, he is speaking about the true self of the world. The world as it can be, as it should be. And Jesus makes clear that the Kingdom of God exists in two realms of reality: the inner life of humans and the physical world that we inhabit. In Jesus's own life and teachings, the Kingdom of God first begins as an inner reality within the hearts and minds of his disciples that is then manifested through them in the physical world.

This inward to outward motion, this is the rhythm of abundance. This is the path to an abundant and meaningful life. Jesus begins his teaching on the Kingdom of God in the Gospel of Luke saying, "They can't say, 'Here it is!' or 'There it is!' You see, the kingdom of God is within you." According to Jesus, the Kingdom of God isn't a thing that appears out of nowhere in the physical world. It's not something that can necessarily be pointed to—instead, it is an inner reality that all of us *already have* and can experience.

The Kingdom of God within us is a way of talking about our truest nature. It's a way of talking about the need for each of us to get beyond the masks, labels, forms, and shadows that we project into the world and identify as "us" and get to the eternal substance, our Divine nature that is the very ground of our being. See, another flaw of our consumerist culture is that we are conditioned to identify ourselves with labels, identities, and what we do. Everywhere we go, it's about *what we do* for work, or our sexuality, or our political party, or whatever else we use to identify ourselves. But do any of these labels actually give even a slightly adequate glimpse into which we are as people?

I fall into this trap all the time. I identify as an author, an activist, a spiritual teacher, and as LGBTQ+. I spend so much of my energy trying to maintain those labels because, I believe, often subconsciously, that those things are fundamentally who I am. I am driven to work harder to make sure those identities stand strong. I have to keep writing endlessly, because if I stop, then am I still an author? That would throw my identity into crisis. So, in order to avoid such a situation, I force myself to keep working harder and harder to look and act like my image.

I am sure you do this, too. If you identify as primarily a parent, you invest endless energies into your kids, and when they fail or don't do what you think they should, you feel threatened and like a failure. Or, if you identify as a political party supporter, and that becomes the fullness of who you see yourself to be, when your party or candidate is threatened or losing, you are thrown into a crisis of identity.

But to do the work of the Kingdom of God is to get beneath all these false identities and masks, to the true eternal nature of who we are. To root ourselves in the reality of the Kingdom of God within, that unmovable, eternal reality that is the essence of who we are. And how do we tap into and ground ourselves in the Kingdom of God within? Only through the hard work of self-discipline and practice.

I am sure that many of us who are involved in organized spirituality already get this. Through practices like meditation, contemplation, prayer, qigong, and other exercises, we move our presence and attention from the temporal identities we have to the serene, constant inner peace that is our truest self. We see that at our core we are all the same. We are all one substance, one consciousness, one reality. The Christian Scriptures call this our "Divine Nature" or "Christ in us, the hope of glory." Our truest and eternal self is love, is God, is consciousness, is pure being. And when we do the daily work of tapping in to our eternal essence and identity, we move about our lives with a grounding and peace that truly passes all understanding. Because when we move from the place of our true self, we are moving from the only place that is truly enduring and eternal. Our beingness cannot be threatened, cannot be changed, cannot be moved. No matter what happens to us in our temporal lives, even if we face death itself, our eternal beingness remains.

So, you can see why beginning in this place of grounding is the perfect antidote to fear, to striving and struggling to create meaning and to identify with those identities that are merely passing manifestations of who we are. In this place of grounding in the eternal, you are lacking nothing and in need of nothing. Only from this place can we taste true enduring joy and peace. As St. Teresa of Avila writes,

> From this [state of inner-grounding] there sometimes
> springs an interior peace and quietude which is full of
> happiness, for the soul is in such a state that it thinks

there is nothing that it lacks. Even speaking—by which I
mean vocal prayer and meditation—wearies it: it would
like to do nothing but love.[7]

Thomas Merton echoes her:

The utter simplicity and obviousness of the infused light
which contemplation pours into our soul suddenly awak-
ens us to a new level of awareness. We enter a region
which we had never even suspected, and yet it is this new
world which seems familiar and obvious. The old world
of our senses is now the one that seems to us strange,
remote and unbelievable. . . . A door opens in the center
of our being and we seem to fall through it into immense
depths which, although they are infinite, are all accessible
to us; all eternity seems to have become ours in this one
placid and breathless contact. . . . You feel as if you were
at last fully born.[8]

This is the "born again" experience that Jesus talks about. The
awakening to the reality of our true nature, beyond the temporal
forms and shadows, where we tap into the very consciousness of
God.

So, the first rhythm, the inward rhythm, of abundance begins
by each day doing work to ground and root ourselves in our true
nature, through the discipline of prayer, meditation, or contemplation. This is a difficult, but essential part of experiencing a life of
fullness and abundance. This is the Kingdom of God within us.

The second rhythm of abundance is the outward rhythm.
This is where Jesus prays, "My God's Kingdom come on earth
as it is in heaven" (Matthew 6:10), or, *May that which is experienced in the inner realm be made manifest in the physical world.*
Jesus shows us that our inner peace precedes outer peace. Inner
abundance precedes outer abundance. But for so many of us
who are deeply invested in developing a rich interior life, we

have often been lax about manifesting what is inside out into the world around us.

This second rhythm is rooted in selflessness, whereas the first one is primarily for the benefit of oneself. The second rhythm is made possible by the first, because in the inward journey we are filled up and strengthened, and the outward rhythm calls for us to empty ourselves for the good of the world. The way that I think about "manifesting the Kingdom on earth as it is in heaven" is looking around me every day for an opportunity to be the hands, feet, voice, or presence of God and love to those who need it most. We are called to live with such awareness in our world that when we identify a place where beauty is being suppressed, where injustice is being perpetuated, where darkness is growing, we choose to enter into those spaces using our time, talents, resources, and energies to set the world to rights. To establish justice, peace, equality, love, and light through one subversive act of love at a time.

Nearly every major spiritual teacher has exhorted us about the importance of humbling ourselves to serve the world. As contemplative Henri Nouwen writes,

> Our humanity comes to its fullest bloom in giving. We become beautiful people when we give whatever we can give: a smile, a handshake, a kiss, an embrace, a word of love, a present, a part of our life . . . all of our life.[9]

One of the most powerful passages from the Christian Scriptures is a hymn that the Apostle Paul quotes about how Jesus lived his life:

> Who, being in the form of God, did not consider equality with God something to be exploited. But He emptied Himself, taking upon Himself the form of a servant, and was made in the likeness of men. And being found in the form of a man, He humbled Himself and became obedient to death, even death on a cross. Therefore God highly

exalted Him and gave Him the name which is above
every name, that at the name of Jesus every knee should
bow, of those in heaven and on earth and under the earth,
and every tongue should confess that Jesus Christ is Lord,
to the glory of God the Father. (Philippians 2:6–8)

This path of self-giving, of humbling oneself for the good of others, this is the path that leads us to exaltation and awakening.

I happen to believe that we are essentially the same as Jesus. He was the firstborn among many siblings, as the Scriptures teach. Therefore, whatever is said of Jesus in this hymn can and should be true of us as well. Though we are in the form of God—we are not called to exploit our Divine nature for our own personal or hedonistic benefit. Instead, we're called to take the fullness that comes from living out of our true self and empty ourselves.

How? By taking the form of a servant. By seeing others as better than ourselves. By seeking to sacrificially give so much that it hurts to bless and extend redemption. This is what Jesus demonstrates, by giving his life for the good of his enemies. And Jesus's example became the pattern for one of the most central Christian practices: communion or the Eucharist.

Every day, I try to enact this outward rhythm by committing to find one moment where I can manifest the power and love of God to someone. I try to make sure it hurts a little, that my sacrifice or altruism isn't done out of my own comfort but calls me out of my comfort zone and is costly. This could look like buying lunch for a person experiencing homelessness, sitting down with a co-worker who you'd normally hate and talking about a struggle they're going through, standing up for a person experiencing marginalization or oppression. It could look like anything. But in order to live in this posture of being an agent of redemption, it's vital that we are aware, that we move from a place of grounding and respond to the nudging of the Spirit within us to pour ourselves out to manifest the rule and reign of God.

When we move in this flow of self-sacrificial giving each day, we experience a deep satisfaction because we are fulfilling one of the reasons we have been created, to be incarnations and co-creators with God in the redemption of the world! We also engage in one of the fundamental laws of the universe: reciprocity. Karma. In giving, we receive, in dying we are reborn.

Every time we sacrificially act as the hands and feet of God, we are putting to death our ego and helping to create a more just world. Every time we extend ourselves through doing subversive acts of love, we are aligning ourselves with the flow of the universe and our created purpose. Every time we stand for justice and righteousness, we will experience more and more abundance and fullness in our own lives and our own world. Through one subversive act of love at a time, we make Jesus's prayer a reality, and manifest the Kingdom of God, the true self of the world, on earth as it is in heaven. This is the outward rhythm of abundant living.

"Seek first the Kingdom of God and everything else you need will come to you," Jesus said. In this, he taught us about the rhythm of abundance. When we make the focus of every day of our lives seeking the establishment of the Kingdom of God within and outside of us, everything else we need will be given to us. When we embrace this fundamental rhythm of being filled up and grounded, and then move out into the world seeking to be channels through which the world is renewed, redeemed, and restored, we experience springs of inner fulfillment and become vessels of light.

This doesn't mean that we won't feel longing or pain or suffering. Of course we will, for that, too, is part of what it means to be a human and a sojourner. Jesus, Buddha, the Dalai Lama, and Dr. King all experienced suffering despite having tapped into this rhythm of abundance and awakening. To be free from longing and suffering cannot be our goal. The goal is instead to find true meaning through discovering of who we truly are and helping uncover the true nature of God's dream for the world. Being filled up and poured out, each and every day—this is the rhythm that brings life and abundance not only to us but also to those around us.

9

The Battle Within

We have all heard it said that we are our own worst enemy, and I know this to be very true. I have too often found myself knowing that I should do something that would benefit me but have chosen to do the opposite. This happens in big things and small. For instance, there are some days I know I should get up, go to a coffee shop, and write so I will meet my deadline. But for some reason, I find myself bogged down and spend the next two hours scrolling endlessly through Instagram or doing just about anything but writing. Or sometimes, I see someone in need, and I know I could help them. But instead I suppress my desire to do good and allow complacency to win. We all struggle with these inner battles.

Within each of us there is a constant tug of war. There is one part seeking goodness, truth, and beauty. There is a godly self that seeks to serve and love and extend grace. And there is another part that is the exact opposite. The side of us that is self-seeking, that is hedonistic, that would rather stay comfortable than grow, that would rather take the shortcut than actually do the work that helps develop us as people. The way the Scriptures speak about this inner battle is by talking about two natures within us—the nature of the flesh and the nature of the Spirit.

The Apostle Paul writes about this in the Epistle to the Romans:

I find the principle with me, the one who wants to do good, that evil is present with me. For I joyfully agree with the law of God in my inner person, but I observe another law in my members, at war with the law of my mind and making me captive to the law of sin that exists in my members. Wretched man that I am! Who will rescue me from this body of death? Thanks be to God through Jesus Christ our Lord! So then, I myself with my mind am enslaved to the law of God, but with my flesh I am enslaved to the law of sin. (Romans 7:21–23)

He is talking about an inner wrestling he is facing between the desire to do good and the actions that he actually does. He is speaking of being enslaved to the "law of sin"—in other places referred to as "the flesh" rebelling against his desire to obey the "law of God"—the Spirit. Within each of us, this war constantly rages.

The Apostle Paul tells us that that the law of God is "written on our hearts" (Romans 2:15). The law of God is the principles that lead to flourishing, whole, and healthy lives. The law of God is the principles that Jesus taught that would make manifest the "the Kingdom of God." Each of us is born with an internal compass that points the way toward abundant life—no one has to tell us that we should love each other—that is built into what it means to be human. No one has to tell us that we should help one another; this is wired into us, too.

The New Testament also describes this as the Holy Spirit indwelling in us. When we commit our lives to follow in the way of Jesus, we remove the blinders of sin and selfishness and open ourselves to listen and be led by the Spirit. The Spirit prompts us and convicts us. The Spirit will prick our hearts and nudge us to act in sacrificial, humble, and loving ways. At the same time, while the Spirit is at work within us, calling us toward holiness, there is another force at work. The law of sin or "the flesh" is the part of us that has been infected with sin: the part that doubts whether the Spirit's leading is the most beneficial path for us.

Do you remember the Garden of Eden story that tells about the introduction of sin into the world? Sin enters when the first humans are led to doubt whether what God said is really best for them. The serpent asks, *Did God really say . . .?*, and the first humans begin to wonder if God's wisdom is really the best path. They begin to wonder whether God is withholding good from them, and they choose to take things into their own hands. They reject God's instructions, and do the very thing He said not to do, warning them that if they did, it would harm them. And, surprise! It turns out that God was right.

This same story plays out within us every day. Each of us has the Spirit within that calls us toward the path of wholeness and holiness. Each of us knows what we should do, what would be best for us and those around us. But we often resist and reject those tugs at our hearts to do good, don't we? This is why spiritual discipline is so important; it allows us to be reminded, refreshed, and recentered so that we can better discern the voice of the Spirit within us when it speaks.

This is also why gathering together in Christian community is essential. Let's face it, when we are not gathering with other believers, being reminded of what we believe in, it is far too easy to fall off the path of following Christ. It is easy to become complacent, falling into unhealthy habits. The very things we know we don't want to do become the things we do. If you want to lose the war within, stop gathering with people around who call you toward Christ. If you want to fall into a pattern of selfishness and sin, disconnect from community. The faith community is meant to strengthen us for the battle against that which calls us away from wholeness. Community helps us hear the voice of the Spirit more clearly, and to tap into that inner wisdom that is the law of God written on our hearts, so that in every circumstance, we know what is good for us and what is right.

If we are honest, as the Apostle Paul was, we often repress the Spirit's voice. We don't rely on the wisdom of our faith. We choose to go our own way, because it's far too easy to believe we know better, and to choose the easiest path over the right path. Like Paul, we suppress what we know to do, and do the opposite. Sometimes, our choice to be selfish instead of selfless may go without any major consequences. Sometimes, we might get ahead when we choose the path of the flesh over the spirit.

But remember: The law of God is not given to us in order to keep God happy. God is not sitting in heaven, watching your every choice, and judging you when you choose the flesh over the Spirit. No, the only one who suffers is you. *You* are bringing judgment on yourself. One small fleshly victory leads to another. It may start off as one night of binge drinking with friends, where you begin to act out and say and do destructive things. When we justify that, then it's easier to justify the next time, and the next. And before you know it, you're trapped in a cycle of addiction.

The Bible's call to fight temptation and sin has nothing to do with being morally superior to others or pleasing God, but rather it's about living a life that leads you toward your highest self. God's call to holiness is intended to steer you toward a lasting sense of joy and meaning in life. The call to fight against our fleshly desires, the impulses we have to seek our own pleasure or our own good above others—it's ultimately for our own blessing. The call to reserve and restrain your sexual and emotional desires—that's not a random moralistic rule; it's a bit of wisdom intended to help you have the most fulfilling and enriching relationships and sex life possible. The call to give of your money isn't a religious rule meant to keep preachers rich; it is a practice to help you realize and remember that money comes and goes, and that when you live simply and give freely, you can actually bring blessing and healing to the world.

But these things are easier said than done, aren't they? Because we're literally at war with our flesh. At war with our inner desires that call us out of sync with the Spirit and out of step with Christ's wisdom. War is an active term; it means that we must be actively resisting, actively guarding ourselves, actively fighting for victory. We must be actively pursuing discipline.

Actively cultivating self-restraint. Actively choosing to remember that just because we have an urge or desire doesn't mean it's good. Paul rightly notes that these battles are primarily mental:

> For I joyfully agree with the law of God in my inner person but I observe another law in my members, at war with the law of my mind and making me captive to the law of sin that exists in my members. (Romans 7:23)

Can you relate to this? I know these are areas I struggle in. It is far easier to be selfish and impulsive. Inside, I really do want to follow God's wisdom. In my mind and heart, I want to follow the path that I truly believe will lead me to abundant life. But "the law of my members" often wins out.

Paul says in his mind he desires to follow God. But in his *members*, he lives out the law of sin. "Members" means body. He is talking about physical pleasure. He's talking about doing things that feel good, even if we know in the long term, they're not leading us toward goodness. This is where the battle lies—that internal truth and desire, and the external allure of pleasure. As a comical example, I have often confessed my love of gummy bears. I know that I shouldn't eat an entire bag of gummy bears. I know I won't feel good afterward. But in the moment, my desire for sensory pleasure—the amazing taste of the sour, chewy, colorful gummy bears—often wins out over what I know is good.

What is it that you fall for? What are the things you do that aren't good for you? What are the areas where you're weakest? These are the areas we need to submit to the wisdom of God. That we need to focus on disciplining ourselves. That we need to share in Christian community so we can have accountability and encouragement from our siblings in Christ, because if we don't do these things which strengthen us in the battle of temptation, we will continue to fall and fail. Our small transgressions will become bigger and the consequences more dire. So, it's important that we prepare for battle now.

For some of us, today needs to be the start of a new way of living. Today needs to be a day where we choose to enter into the battle against our unhealthy behavior or attitudes. Today needs to be the day that we decide we're going to reach out to others and ask for help. Today needs to be the day that we're going to take drastic actions to help us succeed in living in a way that leads us to abundance.

Do you remember how Jesus says to deal with the things that cause us to fall into sin? He says in Matthew 5:30, "If your right hand causes you to sin, cut it off. For it's better for you to lose a hand then for your whole body to perish in hell." Of course, he is using metaphor and speaking in hyperbole, but the principle stands: If something in your life is causing you to fall off the path of following Jesus, you need to cut it out. Remove it from your life. It is often quite painful, but such drastic actions are often necessary for your own well-being. It may be a relationship that you need to sever. It may be that it's time to get rid of the smart phone. It may be that you need to have someone set restrictions on your computer. It may be that you need to move out from that roommate situation. Whatever it is—cut it out. For it's better to go through a little pain now than for you to suffer bigger consequences later. It's better to delay gratification now, for the promise of a fulfilling and meaningful life is far, far better than momentary pleasure.

These are not easy words to write, and I know they're not easy to read, but God desires that you would have an abundant life. Maybe it's time that we commit to waging war against our fleshly desires and unhealthy behaviors. Maybe it's time we commit to not being afraid to speak to one another when we see that we're living in a way that seems to be hurting us or calling us away from Christ.

See, we progressives don't often like to do this kind of thing: we don't like to preach self-restraint because we're afraid of becoming fundamentalist moralists. We're afraid of being seen as judgmental. But it's not judgmental to want the best for ourselves and each other. It's not moralist to choose healthy behaviors over nonhealthy ones and to call those around us to follow in the same path. We must be willing to embrace the value of self-restraint—the ability to reject our desires sometimes because we know that putting our desires off or resisting them is the best thing for us, for others, or because it's the right thing to do.

We must be willing to gently call each other to live lives that are more in line with the will of God—lives that call us toward greater wholeness and holiness. We must be willing to receive that call from others, not as a judgmental word, but from a Spirit of desiring the flourishing of one another. At the same time, let's heed Jesus's own wisdom: let's deal with the log in our own eye before we point out the speck in another's. Let's spend more time focusing on how we can practice discipline, sacrifice, and restraint more than we tell others to.

Remember, we don't walk this path alone. We are called to war against fleshly desires, but we are also given the source of all strength to be our advocate and ally. The more we learn to rely on Christ and his promises, the more victory we will have over the sins that drag us down. The more we meditate on God's word and spend time with God's people, the more we will be pulled away from sinful desires and toward holy desires. Christ through the Spirit and Christ through the church will liberate us, strengthen us, and empower us.

We're given everything that we need to pursue a life of godliness, wholeness, and fulfillment. But we must refuse to fall into the patterns of thinking so common in our world. We must suspend our allegiance to the practices that others tell us will make us whole, and choose to believe God and the two thousand years of Christians who have walked this path before us.

The life we want is within our grasp. A life of wholeness and victory over addictions, compulsions, and unhealthy desires is possible for you. No, more than that—it is probable for you! If you are willing to trust the wisdom of God in this battle toward your highest self.

10

The End of the World as We Know It

Every time our country or the world faces a major crisis, people ask, "Is this the end of the world?"—and every time a crisis occurs, evangelical television networks make millions by preaching that the end is in fact here; that the events taking place were actually prophesied in the Bible; that Jesus is coming back soon, and the final judgment is about to begin.

It is a strange thing that humans are very aware that our lives and our world are fragile. When a crisis emerges, we all ask the big, existential questions: Why are we here? What's the purpose of this all? And ultimately, is there any hope? In moments of upheaval, we become keenly aware that the world as we know it could very well come to an end—that we as a species could actually go extinct—or we may even believe that God is very willing and ready to pour out judgment on the earth. The past twenty years of world history have been filled with moments of crisis and tragedy. And over the past twenty years, we have all probably asked, at times, is this the end?

We all can see that a storm is on the horizon, and there is very little that we feel we can do to stop it. So, we begin to look to the heavens in the hope that if this is the end there will be something better on the other side. And in moments like these, Christians begin to open up their Bibles to that strange and mysterious book in the very back: different Bibles call it different things—some call it the Apocalypse of John, others the Revelation of John, and still others call it the Book of Revelation.

Whatever we call it, in our collective consciousness we have been conditioned to believe that this book says something about how the world is going to end, and we almost automatically begin poring over its words to see if we can decipher where exactly we fit in. That's why it seems fitting, in this moment of global and national crisis, for us as followers of Jesus to look at this book and see what it might say to us in this moment of history.

To start, I want to give you a challenge: as you read this chapter, I want to challenge you to try to forget everything you think you know about the Book of Revelation. Perhaps you've read the *Left Behind* novels or watched the movie. Maybe you remember the book *The Late Great Planet Earth*. Try to forget those images and all that you've heard the TV preachers say about this book.

Let's start at square one, with some background on this book. The Book of Revelation was one of the most disputed texts in the early Christian movement—many churches rejected it as Scripture, believing that it was not truly what it claimed to be, a "prophetic revelation" from Jesus. This fact is not insignificant; as we read the book, we have a right to be skeptical of its claims and its theology, because a good deal of prominent early Christian leaders did as well. In fact, there are a number of denominations today that still do not include Revelation in their versions of the Bible.

We also don't know who wrote the book. The author identifies himself as John, but most scholars are quite certain that this is not John the Baptist or John the Apostle. The author of this book claims to be a prophet; he sees himself in the same lineage as the prophets of the Hebrew Bible, speaking not on his own behalf but as God's mouthpiece. It seems that the author is a leader within the Asian Christian church because he writes to several very real churches on the Western edge of the Roman Province in Asia. He knows these churches intimately and was clearly connected to them in some substantial way.

John finds himself exiled on the Island of Patmos, which today is a beautiful vacation destination, but in his day was a Roman prison island. When elite or high-status individuals were found guilty of a crime in the Roman Empire, rather than be executed like low-class people, they were often instead exiled to an island where they either worked in prison camps or simply were free to live but could never leave. This is what we can deduce about John. He is exiled for life to Patmos for his refusal to renounce Christianity and submit to the emperor as a god.

In the late first and second centuries, Christianity *was* considered a crime in Rome. Refusal to worship the emperor was seen as a seed of political rebellion, and so if Christians did not renounce the central claim of their faith—"Jesus is Lord"—they were often harassed in their local communities, and if that harassment grew, they may well be executed or exiled by the local tribunal.

Most scholars believe that this letter is being written soon after the reign of Emperor Nero, who blamed Christians for a massive fire that burned down Rome, thus beginning a severe persecution of Christians within the empire. Revelation is likely written during the reign of Emperor Domitian, who is known as a bombastic, greedy, and exceedingly cruel emperor who would have happily killed Christians and at very least encouraged their lambasting locally. Domitian, by the way, was such an egomaniacal emperor that he adopted the title Dominus Deus, literally meaning "Lord God," something that very few other emperors did during their lifetimes. Domitian sought to rebuild the importance of the Roman Imperial Cult, which had waned in influence, and demanded worship and adoration as God. So, the Book of Revelation is being written by this man named John, who claims to be a prophet, is a leader in the Asian church, and has been exiled for life to the island of Patmos. He has clearly both experienced persecution and has witnessed it. John claims that the words of Revelation are not his own, but are the words of Jesus Christ. He is just a channel through which Jesus is speaking to the churches.

John is also convinced that Jesus is coming back very soon—within his lifetime. The empire was in a period of upheaval after Nero and in the reign of Domitian, and as Christians were being persecuted, he assumed this was a sign of Jesus's imminent return. The end of the Roman Empire was near as well as the end of the world as he knew it.

He says in Revelation chapter 1:1 that the words of this book "must soon take place"—he meant very soon. Like months. He says in Revelation 1:7: "Look he is coming with the clouds! Every eye will see him, including those who pierced him, and all the tribes of the earth will mourn because of him!" He believed Jesus was coming right now. He even says that some of those who were responsible for Jesus's death would see him come again. Remember, the crucifixion of Jesus likely took place only thirty to fifty years earlier, so it is conceivable that, for instance, a Roman centurion in his twenties at Jesus's death might still be alive to see him return if he did come back. John writes with urgency, telling the churches to get their act together because judgment was around the corner.

This is important to note. Revelation is not about *our* future. It's about the distant *past*—somewhere between 95–96 AD. John was revealing prophecy *for his day*. Many of the images John uses describe events that had *already happened*. The beast he describes is generally accepted by scholars to be an image of Nero. The "Great Whore Babylon" is accepted to be a reference to the Roman Empire and its impending collapse. When he writes about Sodom and Gomorrah, he's referring to Jerusalem, which had in fact been destroyed just like Sodom and Gomorrah when the Romans sacked the city and destroyed the temple in 70 AD.

A proper understanding of Revelation in its culture and context is as a book about real events that have *already* happened. It is true that it ends with a few chapters that describe what has been called "The Final Judgment" in which hell is destroyed and heaven comes to earth; that *is* meant to be an image of the end of time, but remember, the author believed that was going to be happening very soon, tied to all of the other events that were in fact already happening around him. So, all of those TV preachers and titillating novelists, they're simply wrong. They're using these ancient apocalyptic words to play on our fear. They're not being faithful to the text. The only thing they're right about is that the Book of Revelation was about the end of the world—John really believed he was living in the end times and that Jesus was coming back. He believed God's final judgment was about to happen. Just like we do when we're in times of crisis.

The next logical question to ask is, if Revelation is about things that happened two thousand years ago, what relevance does the book have today? Clearly, some of John's prophecies were wrong: Jesus didn't come back; Armageddon didn't happen. So, can this book be useful to us today? I think so.

Revelation is less a prophecy from Jesus than a series of very astute observations about politics, greed, and evil, and how they bring about destruction and pull us away from God's vision of a renewed world. Not only does every generation believe they are living in the end of times, every generation also finds striking parallels between what's happening in the world around them and the Book of Revelation. This is its power. Its use of metaphors and symbols allows it to be a useful tool generation after generation, because what it describes is the cycle of civilization: the ways in which humanity creates kingdoms and governments to bring about peace, but they are corrupted and exploited, and ultimately bring destruction and oppression, and then finally collapse.

John was writing his observation of empire in his day—the greed, the hubris, the oppression. He could see it digging its own grave, and he hoped that when it fell, Jesus was back and could establish God's Kingdom of peace and righteousness once and for all. We too are invited to examine the book and analyze what it has to say about our own world, and there are *so many striking parallels*. There is so much wisdom and warning for us.

With this as the background, I want to explore the content of Revelation 1, which is John's introduction. In Revelation 1:1–19, John introduces us to the image of Jesus that he has in a vision, and this image is nothing short of majestic. Jesus is adorned with long flowing robes, like those of the emperor, and a golden sash. His hair is gray and his eyes burn with fire. Out of his mouth come words that are like a sharp sword, referring to the power of his truth and the authority it commands. When John describes this version of Jesus to the churches in Asia, he is seeking to encourage them, letting them know that Jesus is more majestic, powerful, and glorious than Domitian, who calls himself the "Lord God." John wants us to remember that while Jesus is one who is love, one who desires a personal relationship with us, he is also the king of kings, the rightful ruler of the world.

When John sees the resurrected Jesus, he falls on his face as dead. John is reminding us that Jesus was the peace-loving and caring savior but also that he is a mighty warrior who is willing to fight systems of greed, evil, and oppression in order to set the world right. At once, John falls down and is afraid of the splendor and glory of Jesus. At the same time, Jesus pronounces some of the most powerful words he ever speaks: "Do not be afraid." John had every reason to be afraid: His life was over, he was exiled, cut off from his church who would likely face intense persecution, many of them being killed. The empire seemed unstable and now, he finds himself in a trance in front of Jesus Christ. Fear seems like precisely the right response.

We also have a reason to be afraid, don't we? All is not right in our world. We have a world governed by wicked rulers who have no regard for truth and no respect for law. We have a world that has been stricken by a pandemic that cost millions of lives. Our economy is hanging on by a thread. Racism has been unleashed and affirmed across our country. The earth is heating at record rates, destroying habitats and threatening species with extinction. Black people are being murdered by those charged with protecting them. Today those who claim to follow Christ are not only endorsing but actively participating in all of these evils. None of us knows what is to come, and it very much feels like it could in fact be the end of the world as we know it.

We, like John, have a reason to be afraid, but in the moment of great fear, we are given a gift. We are given an image of Jesus that cuts through the noise of our fear and says "do not be afraid." We hear Jesus say "death itself is in my hand." That's a statement of absolute authority—not even death has power over me, he says. So don't worry about Caesar or the famine, for I am here. I will intervene. I will work to bring redemption. And that, my friends, is the importance of our faith in moments like these. This sort of faith gives birth to courage.

John has been courageous—has is declared the way of Jesus in the midst of an empire that has outlawed Christianity. He has preached the words of Jesus, painting a contrast between the corrupt practices of the empire, and he is suffering for it. In a moment of great upheaval, John sees Jesus in power and glory, and is even more motivated to keep speaking up and proclaiming God's truth. How much more are we called to do the same?

John says in verse 9, "I share with you in the suffering, the kingdom, and patient endurance we have in Jesus." He is saying that the subversive role of Christians in a corrupt world is to live boldly and courageously—making the Kingdom of God a reality in our own lives and societies through demanding justice and living justly, while also knowing that doing so will result in our suffering and will require patience and endurance, just as Jesus lived.

These opening words of the Book of Revelation are intended to expel fear from the hearts of followers of Jesus in the ancient world and in ours. Throughout the book, John doesn't skirt around the evil and suffering that he sees in his world. He doesn't sugarcoat anything. But he invites Christians to subversive faithfulness, knowing that Jesus will have the last word. Revelation is an encouragement to Christians to be willing to stand up, speak up, and live differently when confronted with corrupt rulers, regardless of what the personal cost might be.

These opening words of the Book of Revelation encouraged the earliest followers of Jesus in their darkest moments—it is my prayer that they will encourage us, too, as we face unprecedented challenges of our age. The brave faith of John comes from the fact that he believed that the way of Jesus is the way of victory. That love must win in the end. You see, friends, if our hope is in our own ability to fix the broken system of our nation, or of the world in our own strength, we are doomed. But if we believe that as we work and strive and seek to make a better world, that God is with us, in us, through us, and will bring about victory in the end, then we have reason for great hope. We have a reason to keep our heads held high. We have a reason to keep dreaming and working and believing that the kingdom of this world can become the Kingdom of our Lord—a world of righteousness, equity, and peace for absolutely everyone.

May it be.

11

The Shame Paradox

Have you ever found yourself ashamed of some part of who you are? It could be an identity, be it ethnic, sexual, gender, or national. It could be based on some part of your physical appearance—for me, my "big ears" caused me shame for much of my childhood. It could be shame around your religious identity and how it's perceived by the broader culture. For instance, it's not a wonderful time to be affiliated with the word "Christian" right now in much of our country, right?

In the LGBTQ+ community there is the idea of the "closet," which is simply the reality that many queer people feel the need to hide themselves and their true nature because of familial, cultural, or religious pressure. The closet is created primarily by shame and by a desire to maintain a certain privileged status in society. For many queer people, remaining closeted helps them hold on to "straight" or "cisgender" or "male" privilege. We know that the moment we reveal our truest nature, we will face scorn and marginalization—something nobody wants to experience. And obviously, for many people, closets aren't even an option. Many people find themselves born into a culture that sees some unchangeable part of their identity as inferior, and without revolutionary change, they seem destined to face oppression.

This is the experience of many people of color in our country. You don't need me to rehearse the numbers or stories—we know that if you're a person of color—Black, Brown, Asian—you are more likely to experience wealth inequality, hiring discrimination, harassment from law enforcement, and overt racism. We live in a world of bias, prejudice, and injustice. A world where the elites and powerful often intentionally use and abuse others whom they find to be different or for some reason view as "less-than." This isn't a new reality—it has existed for as long as humans have been around.

There is a short book in the Hebrew Bible called Esther, which tells a fictional story that highlights all sorts of injustices rooted in identity. This book is composed of ten short chapters, and it is the basis of the Jewish feast of Purim. This book was written as a historical novella that represents much of the literature in the Persian culture that it emerges from. So, while its goal is not to recount actual events, like any good story, its purpose is to convey deep truths and principles for us to reflect on and apply.

The word "God" never appears in this text. It is the only book in all of the Bible—with the exception of the Song of Solomon—not to mention God at all. But although it doesn't speak of God, you will see the presence and action of God at work in the story. In other words, God is implied. Like in our own lives—many of us may not mention Jesus every single day; we may not even pray or do anything explicitly Christian; but we live with an awareness of God, assuming that God is with us, around us, and working through and for us. This, I honestly believe, is the mark of a mature faith. A faith that assumes God, rather than seeks to expose God.

The first two chapters of the Book of Esther tell the story of King Ahasuerus and Queen Vashti of Persia. We're told that the king orders a banquet that lasted for 180 days as a display of Persia's grandeur and wealth. Following these celebrations, the king launched another series of celebrations for the people of the citadel of Susa—the men partied with the king and the women with Queen Vashti. At the end of the celebration, the king called for Queen Vashti to be brought over to his celebration so that he could show her beauty off to all the men of the citadel. When Vashti heard this request, she refused to go, resulting in the king becoming incensed with anger. He consults his assistants as to what he should do in response to her disobedience, to which one adviser replies by suggesting that she be removed as queen by the issuing a new royal decree that demands women obey their husbands. The king agrees and issues such a decree for the whole kingdom.

We get a glimpse of the flagrant misogyny at work in this era. Interestingly enough, the story will soon become an early iteration of feminism, but in the beginning, we see nothing but a powerful king who takes a trophy wife and wants to use her as eye candy to gain the admiration of the empire. We also see an incompetent leader—notice that the king doesn't even know what the laws of his own kingdom state, so he calls on advisers to give him options. We also get a glimpse of people who are easily corrupted by power—this adviser named Memucan suggests that the king do away with his wife—first and foremost to ensure that the women of the empire don't start thinking that they can disobey their husbands, and secondly, we will see, because he has his own agenda rooted in racism. We don't know much about Queen Vashti, other than that she was a strong-willed woman, who was likely part of the Persian Empire but spoke a different language than the king. What we can say is that Vashti is an early heroine for the kind of world God is seeking to create. She knew that disobeying the king's orders wouldn't bode well for her, but she did so anyway because she had demonstrated a great deal of self-respect. Vashti refused to be objectified. She refused to allow even the most powerful man in her world to objectify or use her. She was worth more than being an object of lust by onlooking men. Queen Vashti is a heroine; she respected herself even when it cost.

This is a lesson for all marginalized people. None of us are worthy of disrespect. None of us are worthy of being used. None of us are worthy of being subject to others' whims and desires. And we should and must stand up and demand that these Divine laws be honored, even when it may cost us to do so.

People of color are taking to the streets to declare that the kings of this land can no longer objectify and marginalize them. And those of us who are White and White-presenting have a responsibility to demand this with them and for them. Is there a cost? Obviously! But only through subversive, bold resistance can we make God's law a reality.

In chapter 2, we get a profound glimpse at how shame works. After the king issues his decree for women to obey their husbands, he calms down and grows nostalgic for Vashti. When his advisers see this, they send the king's servants to find every eligible woman and bring them to become a part of the king's harem. It is at this point that we are introduced to a Jewish man named Mordecai, who adopted a beautiful girl named Esther into his family. Before Esther is taken by the king's servant to be considered for the harem, Mordecai instructs her to keep her Jewish heritage a secret, fearing that she might be persecuted by the king if her identity was found out. For twelve months, Esther and all the other women were treated with cosmetics and oils to prepare them to be presented to the king, and Esther grew in favor with the king's servants who ensured she received special treatment. During this year, Mordecai waited with much anxiety, wondering if Esther would be selected or perhaps found out to be Jewish.

Eventually, Esther is called in to meet the king, and we are told that immediately, the king found her more desirable than all the other women, so he immediately crowns her queen at a royal state banquet in her honor. Following this celebration, we're told that Mordecai sat at the gate of the palace each day, keeping an eye on Esther's well-being. One day, he overheard a plot by two of the king's servants to murder the king, and Mordecai reports this to Esther, who in turn, tells the king and credits her uncle. The king has the rumor investigated, and once confirmed, has the two officers hung on a pole for all the kingdom to see.

Now that's a cliffhanger.

In chapter 2, besides seeing some more disgusting objectification of women, we see a contrast between a new Jewish woman named

Esther and Queen Vashti: Queen Vashti, for whatever reason, stood in her identity with power and confidence, even though it cost her. Queen Esther, on the other hand, is counseled to hide her identity, to suppress it. On one hand, we cannot blame Esther for listening to the advice of Mordecai. She came from a long line of people who were oppressed because of their ethnic and religious identity. If she had an opportunity to become the queen if only she could "pass" as non-Jewish, that seems like a reasonable thing to do—right?

By denying her identity, she has risen to one of the highest offices in the land. How many modern-day politicians do the same: deny an identity or even adopt a fake identity? It is amazing how many politicians all of a sudden become so Christian in order to ascend to power. Shame locks people in the closet and tells them that they are fundamentally flawed and must suppress their God-given selves in order to get by in the world. And for others, as I said before, the closet isn't even an option; they resign themselves to hopelessness.

This is what Mordecai believes deep down—he is so worried that Esther will be found out that he cannot leave the king's gates. He *wants* to believe she can have a better life but doubts it. This is what Esther believes too—that she's probably not good enough as a Jewish woman to gain the favor of the king. There is shame attached to a fundamental identity.

Contrast that to Queen Vashti who, first and foremost, rose to such a high position *being herself* and then was willing to sacrifice that position to defend her dignity. She didn't speak the right language, clearly, but by standing in her true self, became queen. Then, when the king desired to objectify and devalue her, she refused. She stood firm in who she was. She seemed to know something about living authentically, that being yourself and standing for yourself always yield better results than living in suppression or shame. That transformation of prejudice doesn't happen through secretly conforming to unethical systems and hoping for change, but rather through refusing to be objectified or marginalized. In my own life, this proved true.

As a closeted gay man seeking to be a pastor, I lived with so much inner shame and tension. I knew this was true about myself and that my sexuality wasn't changing, no matter how hard I tried, and I also knew that if I ever spoke that out loud, I would lose my position of privilege. I was supposed to be the next evangelical superstar—my church believed that, my mentors told me that, and I believed that—as disconcerting as the idea of a "religious superstar" is. But being willing to live in the closet, to repress who I was, caused me to live inauthentically in so many other ways. I was filled with constant anxiety and fear. I was plagued with depression, thinking that I was broken and deeply flawed. When you live with that kind of shame and repression there is no way to remain healthy. You will suffer mentally, spiritually, and often your body will begin to break down.

Psychologist Bessel van der Kolk wrote in his book, *The Body Keeps the Score:*

> As long as you keep secrets and suppress information, you are fundamentally at war with yourself. . . . The critical issue is allowing yourself to know what you know. That takes an enormous amount of courage.[10]

When we suppress ourselves, we are warring against what God has created, and to be ourselves authentically does in fact take incredible courage. Again, who can blame Mordecai or Esther for suppressing their Jewish identity; they had seen their people exiled, killed, and made slaves. This was a survival move.

On the other hand, we see Queen Vashti exercising tremendous courage in her embrace and respect for herself. She was willing to sacrifice it all to do what was right, not just for herself but for her people. Clearly, she was seen as an influential woman among women—it's why the king's counselors were so adamant that he make a decree of obedience. She knew that her resistance to subjugation would be a message and green light for other women to stand up for themselves, and it is her example that likely helped propel Esther to bravery later in the story.

Feminist Jewish writer Michel Landsberg wrote of Vashti:

> Saving the Jewish people was important, but at the same time [Esther's] whole submissive, secretive way of being was the absolute archetype of 1950s womanhood. It repelled me. I thought, "Hey, what's wrong with Vashti? She had dignity. She had self-respect. She said: 'I'm not going to dance for you and your pals.'"[11]

Esther hid in shame. Vashti demanded change. These are the two options that the Spirit is presenting us with. If we hope to make changes in our lives or in the world, we must follow Vashti's example. We must move toward reconciling the parts of ourselves that we have been conditioned to despise. We must choose to live in radical authenticity, because doing so will not only help us be healthier and whole, but it can incite a revolution to change society.

I am reminded of a young Black woman named Bree Newsome, who, in 2015 decided that she would no longer put up with living in a state that had a confederate flag waving over it. So, she climbed the flag pole and ripped it down. Just a few years later, states were removing this flag from their buildings and even creating new flags that better represent the dignity and equity of all of their citizens.

I am reminded of Marsha P. Johnson, the Black drag queen who refused to be ashamed of their identity and refused to face brutality at the hands of the police, so they threw a brick through the window of the Stonewall Inn in New York and launched the revolution for queer equity. Now, three decades after their death, LGBTQ+ people have marriage equality, job protections, and a much safer, inclusive country than Johnson could have ever conceived.

These are small actions. Small choices to refuse to marginalize oneself or be marginalized by others. A choice to truly believe, deep in your bones, that you were created just as you are and that all of your quirks, desires, and features are intentionally woven together to make you the person God desired. When you work hard to love who you are and love what you see in the mirror, you will pave the way for others. You will feel more at home in your world, and experience a fuller life.

The call of the Spirit through the example of Queen Vashti is simply that: To show up in the world as yourself. To work to love, and not seek to change or conform, all the unique parts that make you, you. This is especially a word to young people who maybe hear this message a lot, and yet it's so hard to do. When friends in school make fun of you for how you look, for what you believe, for where you live, for who you love, it's hard to just be brave and accept it.

But if you truly believe that God made you with purpose, and that you are who you should be, then I promise that such bravery and courage will make your experience much better, and you will become an example to others who need to know that this is true about them as well. Courageous authenticity is at the core of the Esther story. It's also at the core of following Jesus—the journey toward seeing yourself and the world as God sees it, rather than via the conditioning of our flawed world. Shame seeks to lock us up. Prejudice and racism seek to keep us down, and the best way to break free is to be *brave*. Let's choose to love ourselves, which is one of the foundational commandments of Jesus.

12

God of the Ordinary

I once knew a pastor who wanted to see just how compassionate his congregation was to the "least of these" in their community. He decided to disguise himself and dress up as a person who was experiencing homelessness. He layered up clothing, put on a tangled wig and a long beard, and wrote a cardboard sign that said, "Money for food." He laid on the ground near his church with his sign and a cup, and waited to see how his congregation would respond as they came into church for worship on Sunday morning. As he laid outside, he grew pretty distraught as the first wave of people seemed to divert their eyes from him and keep walking into the church, ignoring his hunger.

Nearly a half an hour passed of people walking by, largely ignoring him. But finally, a family emerged from inside the church with coffee and some pastries. They gently handed him the food, and said "God bless," as they returned inside. Then, dozens of others stopped, offering money, prayer, and an invitation to come inside for the service. The pastor grew overwhelmed and proud of his congregation displaying these simple acts of loving hospitality that our faith requires of us. As the worship service progressed and the time for the sermon arrived, there was an eerie pause and silence. Where was the pastor?

Suddenly, the pastor dressed as a homeless man proceeded from the back of the sanctuary toward the pulpit. The congregation was silent, eyes glued on him. As the man arrived at the microphone, he began to speak, saying "Thank you" to the folks who offered him kindness. He slowly began to remove his disguise. You could hear audible gasps in the congregation as they quickly realized that this individual was actually their pastor.

He spoke about his experiences and many throughout the congregation grew emotional—those who walked by knew they had failed to live up to their faith, and others grew emotional as the lesson became clear, that everyone deserves our kindness and love. For as Jesus himself said, "Whatsoever you do to the least of these, you do to me" (Matthew 25:40).

I think in the same way that this pastor hid himself in order to test his congregation's faithfulness, so does God. In fact, the Scriptures teach us that God seems to like playing hide and seek with us. God disguises Godself, in ordinary people and in ordinary objects, and the test of our faithfulness is whether we have the eyes to perceive God's presence and act accordingly. There is, for instance, a story from the Gospel of Luke (chapter 24) that tells of Jesus disguising himself in many different ways after rising from the dead.

Days after Jesus has been crucified, two of his followers are out walking, reflecting on their pain and shock at seeing him killed. Suddenly, someone approaches them and begins to walk with them. This someone is Jesus, but for whatever reason they don't know it's him. He jumps in on their conversation and begins explaining to them exactly why Jesus had to die, according to the Scriptures.

When they finally get to the house where they are having dinner, Jesus, whom they still don't recognize, says he's going to continue walking, but they insist that he join them for dinner and spend the night. He enters the house and begins dinner with them. He takes the bread, blesses it, and breaks it, just as he had done on that Passover evening when he was last with his disciples. In a moment, as he breaks the bread, presumably saying, "This is my body broken for you," the two men recognize him. And in a moment, he disappears.

I love this story because there are two ways to interpret what is happening, both of which are true and applicable to our lives.

First, perhaps Jesus's disciples were so consumed by their own anxiety and worry that they failed to see that Jesus was with them. Presumably, Jesus looked like Jesus. We don't know what he was wearing, perhaps his beard was cut or hair done differently, but the disciples were so caught up in their despair and worry that when he approached and walked with them, they didn't pay attention to *who* he was. Now, to be fair, Jesus plays dumb with them. He asks them to explain the events that have caused them such despair. And they do. But clearly, they have failed to understand why Jesus was arrested or that he was risen.

Jesus does a Bible study with them. He begins with Genesis and speaks of all the ways the Scriptures prophesied his life and ministry, explaining why he was killed, and that he would rise again. He teaches them, once again, what he had been preaching to them all along. He told them time and time again that this journey would include pain, loss, and suffering—and that ultimately God's love would win in the end. But the disciples did not listen. In three years of following Jesus, they may have listened, but they clearly didn't hear. And even now, when Jesus is standing by their side once again, they don't even realize it.

How true is that for us?

I recently had a conversation with Dr. William Willimon of Duke Divinity School, and I asked him how Christians should be thinking about the COVID-19 pandemic and where God is at in all that is going on in our world. He gave me an answer I wasn't expecting, but one that is deeply true. He said, "Well, Jesus said there was going to be pain and suffering. He went through it and promised that we would, too." He didn't mean that crassly; he was being truthful. Jesus *did* say that in this life we would experience pain and suffering. Jesus *did* say that we would have crosses to bear. Jesus said that over and over again, and yet we remain surprised whenever such pain and suffering emerges. We are no better than the disciples, in this way.

We act as if God has somehow abandoned us, but the truth is that God prepared us for this. God prepared us and promised us that, even in darkness, his light would guide and his hand would provide for us. But we often get in the mind-set of privilege that says, "That will never happen to me." We, for some reason, believe that we are special and exempt from the promise of pain, loss, and suffering. We have more faith in our own exemption to such world-shaking experiences than we do in the clear words of Jesus. We allow our own anxieties and worries to pull us away from what is true. And we miss God. We miss our chance to learn. We miss an opportunity to exercise our faith and trust in God's love for us. We choose to be so consumed by the "what ifs" rather than opening our eyes to see God with us right now.

None of us are exempt from this kind of spiritual amnesia, and God doesn't judge us for our spiritual unfaithfulness either. Instead, he provides the opportunity for us to hear the truth again and be reminded of what we should expect in life and how we should respond. Jesus explained it to these disciples all over again. He graciously taught them the same truths they had heard dozens of times. You see, God is patient with us. But what is better than hearing truth again and again is believing it and walking in it.

In this strange time of loss, pain, fear, and unknowns, the first lesson from this story is to pivot from our posture of anxiety toward a posture of faith. To turn from shock and bewilderment to acceptance and responding like Jesus. Our lives have been changed by this virus. Our world is being reshaped. The question is whether we will be aware enough of God's presence and work in and through this moment to participate with God in bringing about healing, hope, and redemption, or whether we will be consumed by our fear.

The second perspective we can take with this is that God hides Godself in and through ordinary life. This passage literally says that the disciples were "kept from recognizing him," which seems to suggest that Jesus is intentionally trying to hide his identity. One way that this is interpreted is that the man walking on the road with them is truly just another traveler—someone who is just hearing the news about Jesus and yet is well versed in Scripture and explains the truth to the disciples.

The message here could be that God is present in and through everyone and everything, but we often do not have the eyes to see it. Perhaps this is what Jesus meant when he said, "Whatever you do to the least of these you do unto me." Obviously, when we don't help the poor, we're not literally withholding from the physical man named Jesus who was born two thousand years ago, but we are apart from his spirit and his presence, which holds all things together. There is no one and nothing in our world that is not infused with God's presence. This is precisely what the theological term "omnipresence" means, that there is nowhere we can be or go that God is not, for "in God we live."

Perhaps Jesus was with that strange traveler on the road, and perhaps Jesus used that traveler to open the eyes of his disciples while also allowing the disciples to be faithful, as well, by inviting the traveler in for the meal and a place to stay. And perhaps, when the traveler broke the bread, they were reminded of Jesus and that Passover feast before his arrest, where he embodied love and generosity. As they saw the stranger breaking and sharing bread, perhaps they saw Christ—not physically, but spiritually. They recognized that Christ was indeed with them, in a stranger, in a simple loaf of bread, and they realized that he was truly risen and all of creation was filled with his risen presence.

If we interpret the story in this way, then the challenge for us is to work hard at opening our spiritual eyes to see Christ in the face of everyone we encounter, in every mundane moment, in every grain of sand. This requires a shift in our mind-set, reminding ourselves daily to stop, breathe, and perceive God's presence. And to continue to return to regular practices that open us up see God.

I'll be the first to admit that I am the worst at self-discipline. I am the worst at committing to do something every single day. When I was young, I never missed doing my devotions—meaning reading my Bible—because I believed that if I didn't, somehow God would judge me, or I would fall into the devil's traps. Now that I no longer believe in a God like that, now that I know that God loves me and is with me, I often take that grace and freedom for granted. I don't develop healthy spiritual practices like meditation, prayer, or Scripture reading. And yet these are the tools our faith tradition has given us to grow and to become increasingly aware of God's presence.

If we don't train ourselves, we will be like the disciples: God will be right in front of us and we will not be able to perceive God. We will be like a GPS that is out of sync with the satellites, being led all over the place except for the direction that connects us to God's Spirit. If we aren't committed to spiritual exercise, then we will not be able to experience the power and presence of God in the mundane moments of our day. And a life disconnected from and blind to God is a life that quickly fills with cynicism, anxiety, and despair.

At the end of that story in Luke chapter 24, we're told that Jesus's disciples are *still* hiding in an upper room confused and anxious. Jesus has already risen—he has already appeared to them—and they still are blind to his ongoing presence with them. How much truer is this for us? When was the last time you felt the presence of God? When was the last time you saw God moving in your life? The more we walk in faith and exercise our spirits, the more we will see God. Because God is at work, Christ is in our midst, and God is closer to us than our very breath. The question is, can we see God? Does God fill us with peace and hope? Or are we still locked in our own dark tombs of despair?

Imagine what it would be like to grow in constant awareness of God. Imagine what our lives could begin to look and feel like. God has given us moments in this crisis to work on developing our spiritual discipline and opening our eyes to see more clearly. Let's not waste this moment.

13

The Call of God

Have you ever had a dream or a vision that you sat around and mulled over for years? Maybe it was when you were younger—a vision for what profession you wanted to be when you grew up. Maybe it was a basketball player. Maybe it was a doctor. Maybe it was a singer. You had an idea of what you wanted to do with your life, and it burned within you.

Every time you would see a doctor or basketball player or singer on TV, you thought to yourself, one day that will be me. Maybe you spent time playing make-believe, pretending to be that thing you felt drawn to be. When this vocation (this calling) catches you, it can begin to consume you, especially if you have a personality like mine. When I feel called to something, I throw myself at it and will work and work until I make it a reality.

Often, when you have a calling or dream like this you begin to share it with anyone who will listen. "I'm gonna be a singer one day," you told your parents. All of your friends at school knew you wanted to be a marine biologist. And for some of us, that sense of calling toward a vocation doesn't go away; it follows us into our twenties and may actually materialize in our lives.

Whether or not this was your experience, all of us have had that overwhelming sense that there was something we were sup-posed to do. Whether it was something big like a vocation or something small like an idea to make something at work more efficient, when we have that sense of calling, it's hard to resist it. And when we finally do manifest whatever it is that we're called to do, there is usually a sense of deep relief and satisfaction, maybe even celebration.

Throughout Jesus's life, his sense of calling seems to be over-whelmingly clear. From the time he was a young boy he was lean-ing into his call to be the Messiah, the liberator of the world. Outside of our Bible there are actually other sacred texts held by other Christian traditions around the world that tell stories of the child Jesus struggling and straining to become the Messiah he felt called to be. If you are interested, you should really go read "the infancy gospels," because some of the stories are absolutely hilarious. For instance,

> One day a child was running through the village and ran into Jesus's shoulder. And Jesus was provoked and said unto him: You will not continue to run on your way! And immediately the child fell down and died.
>
> When the people saw this, they exclaimed: From whom was this child born, for that every word he pro-claims comes to pass? And the parents of the child who died came to Joseph, and blamed him, saying: Your child Jesus can no longer live in our village: or at very least, you must teach him not to bless or curse anyone, for he is killing our children!
>
> And Joseph called the young Jesus over and admon-ished him, saying: Why are you doing these things that are causing people to hate and persecute us? But Jesus said: I know that your words are not truly yours: never-theless, for your sake I will hold my peace: but they shall bear their punishment.
>
> And straightway those that accused him were smitten with blindness. And they that saw it were deeply afraid

and perplexed, and said concerning him that every word
that he spoke, whether it was good or bad, was a deed
and it came to pass.[12]

That is pretty intense, isn't it? These stories are likely not his-
torically true, but they paint a picture of a young Jesus who is
struggling to understand what it was like to have a calling from
God to be the Messiah. The authors wanted us to see Jesus as a
boy who was wrestling and growing into his Divine identity.

Throughout the Gospel accounts of Matthew, Mark, Luke,
and John—the ones that made it into the official "canon" of the
Bible—we hear Jesus time and again telling his disciples who he is
and what he is called to do in the world. Time and again he tells
them that he has been sent to bring about something called the
Kingdom of God, and that in order to do so, he will have to be
arrested, crucified, and rise again from the dead. Time and again,
he tells his disciples what kind of king God has anointed him to
be—not one who rules with a sword and with war, but one who
rules through sacrifice and unconditional love. Time and again
Jesus is living into his calling and clearly saying who he has been
designed to be, and just as frequently, his disciples seem to refuse
to hear him. They continue to believe that he is going to be the
Messiah they want, one who will fight the Roman Empire, will
overturn the rule of King Herod, and set the Jewish people free
from oppression and persecution.

How many of you have ever gone through this same frustrating reality? When you have told people who God has made
you to be or you have expressed a deep sense of calling, only to
be told that it'd be better for you to go another way or to take a
more conventional path? How many of us have tried and tried
to express our unique calling or identity only to be ignored or
forced into somebody else's boxes? Oftentimes in life, the very
thing God is calling us to do, or the very person God has created
us to be, calls us into conflict with everyone else's desire for us.

Sometimes, it even comes into conflict with the life that we desire for ourselves.

In our society, having financial stability is one of our highest goals, isn't it? But what if we have been created and wired to pursue a profession or a goal that will move us further away from financial stability? Conventional wisdom says that the risk isn't worth it. But God's wisdom says that when you take a step of faith and make a sacrifice to obey God's calling for your life, blessing lies around the corner.

In our society, we have been told that people should act, look, and be a certain way. But what if God has crafted you with a unique and different expression of human creativity? Conventional wisdom says to stick to the status quo. God's wisdom says to let your uniqueness shine forth, because when you do, you bring glory to your Creator.

I believe that for most of us, multiple times throughout our lives, God is going to put a calling within us. A calling to be something, or to go somewhere, or to do something. And while we might wrestle with some fear and anxiety, a part of us will burn on the inside, wanting to make the calling a reality. If we really catch the flame, we might begin to tell other people about our calling, and when we do, they might look at us like we're crazy. But when you have a calling or an anointing from God, you shouldn't expect finite human minds to grasp it at first. Sometimes, you're going to have to take a step of faith apart from everybody else before people really begin to see God working in you.

The Palm Sunday story is exactly this. Jesus is wrestling with his calling to be the Messiah; his circle of friends fail to understand and see his calling for what it was. On Palm Sunday, for the first time, Jesus takes a tangible, physical step toward the hard path that he knows he is being called to. And for the first time, people's eyes and hearts are open to see him as the person God has created and anointed to be the Messiah.

This is how the story goes in the Gospel of Matthew 19:29–44:

As Jesus came near Bethphage and Bethany, towns near the hill called the Mount of Olives, he sent out two of his followers. He said, "Go to the town you can see there. When you enter it, you will find a colt tied there, which no one has ever ridden. Untie it and bring it here to me. If anyone asks you why you are untying it, say that the Master needs it."

The two followers went into town and found the colt just as Jesus had told them. As they were untying it, its owners came out and asked the followers, "Why are you untying our colt?"

The followers answered, "The Master needs it."

So they brought it to Jesus, threw their coats on the colt's back, and put Jesus on it.

As Jesus rode toward Jerusalem, others spread their coats on the road before him. As he was coming close to Jerusalem, on the way down the Mount of Olives, the whole crowd of followers began joyfully shouting praise to God for all the miracles they had seen.

They said: "Hosanna! God bless the king who comes in the name of the Lord! There is peace in heaven and glory to God!"

Some of the Pharisees in the crowd said to Jesus, "Teacher, tell your followers not to say these things." But Jesus answered, "I tell you, if my followers didn't say these things, then the stones would cry out." (CSV)

All of Jesus's life and ministry has brought him to this point. He has spent most of his life living and preaching outside of Jerusalem, the capital city, the center of Jewish religious, social, and political life. And now, during the time of Passover, Jesus sets his sights on Jerusalem.

Jesus knows that it was prophesied that the Messiah must enter the holy city of Jerusalem and proclaim the Gospel in order to reach the whole Jewish world. Jesus also knew that if he entered Jerusalem, a highly secure city, and proclaimed the potent message of God, which condemned the religious and political rulers, he was also likely to be killed.

It was one thing to utter challenges about the religious and political rulers out in the countryside. If the officials heard of this happening, they could likely write it off as some crazy hick out in the fields saying ridiculous things. But to come to Jerusalem was to confront the establishment face to face. To come to Jerusalem and proclaim that you are the Messiah, the true King, was to face certain arrest and likely death. Then again, Jesus knew that this was where his life was heading.

Time and time again, Jesus told his disciples that a time was coming when he would be handed over to the religious and political rulers for the message he proclaimed, and that he would be killed. He also told his followers that they should not fret or lose faith when this happens—for God would raise him from the dead. But because Jesus's calling seemed so outside of the ordinary, because it did not fit with his disciples' paradigm of who the Messiah was supposed to be, they didn't hear him. Or, they heard him say these things, but they weren't truly listening.

The passage begins by Jesus telling two of his disciples to run off and find a donkey and bring it to him to ride on. He asked them to do this because he knew what the Hebrew Bible said: it predicted that the Messiah would ride into the city of Jerusalem on a donkey. The Prophet Zechariah wrote nearly eight hundred years earlier:

Rejoice greatly, Daughter Zion! Shout, Daughter Jerusalem! See, your king comes to you, righteous and victorious, lowly and riding on a donkey, on a colt, the foal of a donkey. (Zechariah 9:9)

Throughout the Hebrew Scriptures, the people were told that the Messiah of God would be humble; he wouldn't ride into Jerusalem on a large white stallion like the kings of other empires. He would come lowly and riding on a donkey, not even a donkey but a colt, the foal of a donkey. This prophecy is trying to communicate that God isn't seeking to save the world through power, dominance, and might, but through the unexpected way—through weakness, sacrifice, and love. But again, the people in their selective memory chose to forget these prophecies and longed for a Messiah who would come in earthly power. Jesus knew what he was doing. He was finally about to step into his calling, into his truest identity fully for all to see.

So, they bring Jesus a donkey to ride down the Mount of Olives to the east gate of Jerusalem. The journey was a short one. By car it's four minutes today. On foot, it would take you thirty minutes. On donkey, it probably took about twenty. This gate, the eastern gate, is the closest gate to the temple, which is the center of Jewish political and religious life. So as Jesus rides into the city, he is entering right into the heart of everything. The heart of power. The heart of religion. The heart of social life. And remember, it is Passover, so thousands of Jews have come from all around Israel to Jerusalem to partake in this holy celebration at the temple. Imagine that coming through the east gate would be like walking into the middle of Times Square on New Year's Eve. It is packed. There's so much going on. And the text tells us that as Jesus began his journey toward the gate, his disciples finally realize what's happening.

They realize he is fulfilling the prophecy of Zechariah. They realize he is stepping into his full identity as the Messiah. And they aren't the only ones. Apparently, a great throng of people join in to this procession, throwing their coats on the path before Jesus and waving palm branches exclaiming, "Hosanna! Blessed is the king who comes in the name of the Lord!" When people see his disciples doing this—throwing cloaks and waving branches, and proclaiming

"Hosanna!"—they know what is happening. This behavior in Jewish culture was fit only for the king of the Jewish people. And they expected that this would be the Messiah, the one who would liberate them from oppression. So, they join in the exclamation. For the first time, Jesus embraces his calling and his identity.

For the first time, he fully and publicly allows himself to be identified this way. And as he does, the people rejoice. Now, the word that is proclaimed as Jesus rides into Jerusalem is "Hosanna," which in Hebrew has two meanings. The first meaning is "Save us!" It is a cry from an oppressed people, yearning for someone to liberate them, to bring them justice. But by the first century, the word Hosanna had also evolved in the vernacular Aramaic, in which it was also used, to be a cry of praise, meaning "Salvation is here!" It is a recognition of God's faithfulness to show up and to save his people from destruction.

Hosanna is the cry for God to save us from brokenness, evil, and injustice. And it is a proclamation of God's faithfulness—that the moment we call upon God for salvation, he is swift and gracious to bring us salvation. In this prophetic moment in the Jesus story, the history of the Israelites is coming to its culmination. For nearly one thousand years at this point, the people had been crying *Hosanna* as a prayer. "God save us!" God had sent many teachers, kings, and prophets to help guide the people, but none offered the salvation that Israel really needed—a salvation not only from physical oppression, but from spiritual oppression. And many times, over the one thousand years, they lost faith.

How many of us have gone through the same thing? We've been crying out to God *save me, show up, deliver me, help me*, and it seems like our prayers are bouncing off the ceiling and falling right back down to earth. But, you see, I believe that every trial we face, every fire we walk through, every hard time that emerges in our lives is meant to help teach us, guide us, and refine us—to prepare us for God's deliverance and salvation.

Sometimes, God allows us to face trials and tribulations to break our hard hearts and hard heads. Sometimes, God doesn't give us what we ask for in our timing or in our way because God knows we're not ready to receive it. And in those periods of trial, we are called to keep crying out "Hosanna!"—save us. Trusting in God. Listening for God. Looking for what God might have to say to us.

Signified by Jesus, the promise of God is that the Spirit will show up in our lives and guide us. That the Spirit of God will embrace us in unconditional love and guide our steps. When we call upon the name of the Lord and patiently, faithfully wait, we are promised that salvation *will* come! That is good news. And that is a word for someone today. Keep crying out to God. Open your heart to God. Your prayer will turn into celebration. God stands ready to save you! Now notice that as Jesus steps into his identity as the Messiah, and as the people celebrate with cries of Hosanna, not everyone is happy about it.

The Pharisees, who are the religious ruling class in the temple apparently stop Jesus as he's entering in the city gates and say to him, "Teacher, rebuke your disciples!" Why? Because unless Jesus rebukes them and says, "Don't call me the King. Don't call me your salvation," then Jesus is in effect claiming to be what they say he is—the Messiah who would undermine the authority of the religious authorities in the temple as well as the Roman authorities. But Jesus doesn't rebuke the people. With a sparkle in his eye and sarcasm in his lips, he snaps back, "If I tried to stop these people from celebrating, the rocks would cry out instead!" In other words, he's owning who he is. He's owning God's calling on his life. He's stepping into his full identity, regardless of the cost.

Notice that as he does this, some people rejoice, and some critique him. The same is true for our lives. When we fully step into the calling on our lives, there will be those who rejoice to see us living into who God made us to be, but there will also be those who critique us and scheme against us. How should we respond? Just like Jesus—with subversive joy.

If we don't follow God's calling, live into who God made us to be, the rocks would cry out on our behalf. Creation would be missing something crucial. God has uniquely created and called each of us. We can't allow the naysayers to keep us from being who God made us to be. We need to embrace our callings and our identities, knowing that like Jesus, there may be a cost.

It may cost some relationships. It may cost financial security. It may cost material possessions. It may even cost our lives. But the cost is worth it, to live into who God made us to be. To live in alignment with our purpose. To live in the Divine flow of God's creative intent.

God has created you with a purpose, friend. Do you believe that? God has created you and given you a calling. There is a point and purpose to your life. And like Jesus, we may spend decades wrestling with fully owning who God has made us to be. Maybe the timing wasn't right. Maybe we had some more things to learn to be prepared. But there will come a time when you're called to take a step of faith. To own who you are and others to see God's calling and anointing on your life. Some will celebrate you and will see God's anointing upon your life and plan. Others will critique and discourage you. Listen to the voice of God. Listen to the voice of the ones cheering, because those are the voices aligned with God's purposes.

Jesus shrugs off the Pharisees. He embraces the encouragement. He embraces his calling, even though he knows it's coming at a high cost. For Jesus, his calling is to be a different kind of king, one who brings salvation to the world, who breaks the power of sin and death through his life and death. His calling is to be the incarnation of Hosanna, bringing salvation to his people. That's the purpose and point of his life. And on that original Palm Sunday, he embraces it fully and finally. May we follow in his path and embrace all that our Creator has called us to be as well.

14

Divided We Fall

We stand in a liminal space today, in a time of tension, transformation, and transition. It has been said before, but it bears repeating, that the divisions we are experiencing now are the greatest they have been in our country since the Civil War. As a people, we have made apparent the very different visions we desire for the future; we've revealed that we have fundamentally different understandings of who we are now as a people. To say the division is between left and right is far too simplistic.

Our political system is broken, because our political system is simply us. We are the ones who elect representatives and platforms. We are the ones who shape policies and the trajectories of our communities. Politics, from the ancient Greeks who taught it to us, means nothing more than "the affairs of the city," the decisions of the people about how to organize and govern themselves.

Christianity teaches that all of humanity is infected by sin, which is characterized by greed and selfishness. So, it is no surprise that every time humanity has tried to govern ourselves, we have stumbled over our own brokenness, as well as the greed and self-interested attitudes that reign within us. But Christianity also gives us hope that through the power of God's Spirit at work within us and in our world, we can reorient ourselves away from greed and toward generosity, away from selfishness and toward compassionate care of others. When we orient ourselves in that direction, we will begin to experience a new reality that Jesus called the "Kingdom of God," or the way God intended the world to function.

In this sense, the promises and policies that come from the lips of political candidates are nothing more than a reflection of what we desire for ourselves and what we actually care about. The way we vote reveals what we believe about who we are as people and what we're capable of accomplishing together. Because this is true, there is good reason to have a bit of anxiety around moments when elections feel threatened. We should feel deeply passionate about the direction we desire to see our nation move in, and we should be concerned if there is a possibility of it moving away from those ideals and values. And when the posture and policies are as severely different as they are in our country today, our anxiety should be all the more heightened.

It would be easy to say, "No matter what happens, God is in control." I am not going to say that. It would be easy to say, "Jesus was not engaged in politics," but that is untrue. It'd be easy to make a plea for unity, regardless of the results of our elections, but that would be disingenuous. Division is not, in and of itself, wrong. And forced unity, when there are such stark moral divides, can be incredibly evil. Our rabbi, Jesus, proclaimed as much when he said in Matthew 10:34: "Do not suppose that I have come to bring peace to the earth. I did not come to bring peace, but a sword."

As much as many Christians have struggled to make Jesus into an apolitical Savior, it's impossible to read the story and teachings of Christ, with a knowledge of their historical context, and not see how politically divisive Jesus was. Throughout the Gospels, Jesus talks about the division he will bring as he separates the sheep from the goats and the wheat from the chaff. He says he's come to divide us with a sword—commonly understood not to be a claim about violence but a reference to the truth. Jesus teaches that the truth sometimes divides us like a sword. Jesus also tells us to expect that when we live in alignment with truth and seek to tell the truth, peace may not be possible. Because truth is disruptive. It shines a light on things hidden. It either convicts or consoles us, depending on which side of its judgment we find ourselves.

It should not be a surprise that we are divided. It should not be a surprise that folks on both sides of the political aisle claim the name of Jesus as a means of legitimizing their perspectives. And we shouldn't expect that we will be truly united any time soon—a conversion will need to take place for that to happen.

Christians believe that we have been made in the image and likeness of a God who is fundamentally free and therefore we too have been granted a measure of freedom in how we orient our lives and the direction that we move our society in. This is why the Scriptures are filled with commands to choose and to repent, which literally means to decide to change the direction you're walking. Jesus taught that humans were ultimately given two paths to walk: one that leads toward abundant life and another that leads toward destruction.

In Matthew 7:12–14, Jesus says,

> So in everything, do to others what you would have them do to you, for this sums up the Law and the Prophets. Enter through the narrow gate. For wide is the gate and broad is the road that leads to destruction, and many enter through it. But small is the gate and narrow the road that leads to life, and only a few find it.

The context of this famous passage isn't heaven and hell. Jesus isn't talking about eternity. He's not talking about believing the right things. He is talking about how we live our lives in the here and now, and the results of our choices. Directly after summarizing all of the teachings of the Hebrew Bible as "Do to others what you would have them do to you," Jesus says, "Enter through the narrow gate."

The context is that the narrow gate that leads toward abundant life is characterized by a commitment to do unto others. He's saying that if you want to flourish in this world, take the difficult path of equity. The path that seeks to level the playing field, the path that ensures that the same good that we desire for ourselves is extended to everyone else. He contrasts this with what he suggests is the easier path, the broad road, the wide gate that leads to destruction, again, not in hell but in this world. He says many, if not most, people will choose to walk that road, and in so doing they will bring destruction to their world.

Jesus tells us that there is a fork in the road. There is a binary choice. One path is easy, but it will result in destruction. The other path is hard, but it will create the more just world that we all ultimately desire. Jesus calls us to resist our broken nature—to rise above our sinful impulses to put our own self-interest above the well-being of others, to choose to walk the path that he himself embodied. But even as he spoke these words, he knew that only a few would find it. Only a few would choose this path.

Jesus, two thousand years ago, told us that we have a choice to make every day in our actions, in our attitudes, and yes, in our politics. Will we be guided by the law of God, summed up in love thy neighbor or will we be guided by love thyself? Love thyself, on its own, will always lead us to destruction. Love thyself, accompanied by love thy neighbor, will always lead us to flourishing. And every day, every human is faced with this simple yet monumental choice: will I live for myself or for others?

This is why Jesus says in the verses directly following these teachings, "By their fruits you will know if they are truly my disciples" (v. 16) and "Not everyone who says to me, 'Lord, Lord,' will enter the kingdom, but only the one who does the will of my Father" (v. 21). He is saying that those who bring about society's healing and flourishing will be clearly marked by good fruit. He is saying that those who bring about society's destruction will be marked by their eagerness to claim the name of the Lord with their lips but who do not actually do the work to make God's Kingdom on earth as it is in heaven.

The contrast Jesus paints couldn't be starker. The posture of life that Jesus calls his disciples toward couldn't be clearer. Our destiny is our choice. The future of our country is our choice. The future of our lives is our choice. The future of the human species is our choice. As much as we long to be consoled by religious affirmations of God's sovereignty and control over the world, the message Jesus communicated was exactly the opposite. He says, in effect, "God has given you control. Now choose the direction you'd like to go." Will you orient yourself toward the equity, flourishing, and well-being of your neighbor or will you orient yourself toward your own well-being, regardless of what happens to your neighbor?

This is the singular principle that should guide Christian politics, ethics, and social positions. Is it rugged individualism, or is it collective prosperity? Is it pulling ourselves up by our bootstraps or is it giving a hand up to our neighbor in need? Our choice determines our direction—toward life or toward destruction.

15

Diving into Doubt

In a world such as ours, where things are constantly changing and we feel as if we have to continually be on our toes, we crave certainty and stability. We crave a solid foundation on which to stand, that quells our inner anxieties and fears. Something to soothe us and help us feel like everything will be okay. For many of us, this is where religion comes in.

Religion offers simple, concrete answers to life's biggest concerns. It offers simple practices that promise to secure God's favor and assurance of eternal well-being. When I came to faith, that's certainly what I was looking for. As a boy, I had no sense of stability in life. My inner world was plagued with an anxiety disorder that was growing increasingly out of control. My anxiety was so overwhelming that I would hide in a closet at lunch time every day; going into the cafeteria would cause me so much panic that I would much rather sit and eat alone with myself and God.

The future, to me, seemed dim. I didn't believe I had much of an opportunity to do anything worthwhile, to go anywhere with my life. My home life was often turbulent: financial instability, and the state of my parents' relationship and our well-being at home were always in question. So, when someone offered me stability, certainty, assurance for the first time, I ran to embrace it. And because I was discovering this faith in the context of a fundamentalist church, certainty was the language that I was being sold.

I remember my pastor saying from the pulpit, "It's not that I am closed-minded, it is that I've already found the answer." I would parrot that phrase to anyone who critiqued me for my narrow-minded, rigid arrogance as a teenager who believed he had found the final answer for all of life's biggest questions. It's easy to laugh at that kind of faith or to make fun of it. But the truth is, it's really attractive. It's really important for some people; it was for me.

If I didn't have that injection of certainty into my young life, I don't know that I would have been able to form and grow in a healthy way. And there are a great many people around us who live lives that are incredibly traumatic and turbulent, who cling to a rigid religious worldview because it's the *only thing that gives them stability.*

It's only from a place of relative privilege that fundamentalism of some sort is not needed. If you are economically stable, relationally secure, and have a sure vision of where your life can go, you don't need these stabilizing forces. But for those who do not have that, some form of stabilizing ideology becomes essential—religious or otherwise. But of course, there is a flip side to this as well.

As humans grow and develop, our levels of consciousness are meant to develop as well. We grow and begin to experience the world, experience different realities and perspectives, and then we begin to ask questions about our inherited framework. We begin to doubt. Fundamentalist systems *hate* doubt. They label it as demonic. They call it destructive to your soul. And their reason for doing so is obvious: once you've established stability and believe you've arrived at the answers to life's questions, there is no reason to doubt. Doubt only seems dangerous. It only seems to inject that fear and uncertainty back in to your life. Who would want that?

This is where language of "heretics" begins to emerge, as groups begin to exclude and marginalize those in their midst who dare to doubt, who seek to destabilize the lives of the rest of the group. They push them out. By the way, this doesn't only happen in religious groups. There are very militant atheists who cling to the idea that there is no god and no ultimate meaning, and are unwilling to allow for doubt or questions to be raised against their ideology either, because humans long for certainty. We all long for the answers. We long to know deep in our bones what is true about us, our lives, and our world. We long to feel affirmed by our group and by our God. We long to fit in. We long to have our identity anchored in a community that embraces us.

But there comes a point in many of our lives where the answers of our community are called into question. Where the things we've believed are absolutely true may not, in fact, be so absolute after all. Often, there is an event or series of events that happens that begins to put cracks in the foundation of our faith. There is a moment where we realize the thing we worshiped as God was not God, but an idol—a collection of beliefs and projections that could never actually bear any resemblance to the Divine. Maybe there is a moment of personal tragedy or crisis that is flatly unjust and wrong and what we thought of as God is absent. Maybe it's a moment of learning, where we stumble on some universally accepted facts that contradict what we have been believing and we feel foolish or duped. In these moments of doubt, we typically grow more and more hurt and cynical, and reject the whole system that we once clung to so tightly as wrong, unjust, and perhaps evil.

This is what happens to many college-age kids who leave their religious bubble and very quickly find out just how limited their world was. They reject faith and run far from it. But there's also another path. It is often a path that takes more time; it usually emerges a little bit later in life, after one has deconstructed a faith and walked without it for some time, as moving from the rubble of myth can emerge the flower of curiosity. Curiosity that accepts that certainty is an illusion, but the quest for meaning, for purpose, for God isn't a dead end. Curiosity that begins to be playful with doubt and beliefs, with a bit of humility attached to it. Curiosity that is willing to embrace questions as a necessary part of being a finite being in an infinite universe.

There is a story in Scripture that reflects the reality of doubt in the Gospel of Matthew, chapter 27. Here, there is a man named Jesus. He believed he was the son of God. He believed he was chosen and walked in God's favor and truth. And after a few years of living life as a teacher, one who opened many people's eyes to God's true will and way, Jesus finds himself arrested, convicted, and being executed. Why? Because he caused others to doubt their system of certainty. He encouraged people to be skeptical of the motives and intentions of their religious systems. He invited them to be creative and innovative with their beliefs and adherence to religious rules. He warned people to be wary of Caesar's claim that he was God. He invited them to be skeptical of the ability of humans to create the ultimate Divine Kingdom, as Rome was seeking to do. And his injection of curiosity and doubt into their minds posed a threat to the security and stability of the system.

So, they exile him. They marginalize him, and they kill him. And as Jesus is hanging on a tree, dying because of his willingness to be curious and to ask the hard questions, he himself faces the most fundamental doubt that all of us face. Doubt of God's very existence. Matthew 27:46 says that as he hung, bleeding and dying, Jesus cried with a loud voice saying, "My God, my God, why have you forsaken me?"

Jesus, who spent his life encouraging others to be curious and doubt, in this moment of deep need, of tremendous injustice and pain, himself cries out in a voice of doubt. How could you forsake me? God, are you even there? This is one of the most profound religious stories ever told because, in it, the one who is called the one true God doubts their own existence. According to orthodox Christian theology, here on the cross, God doubts God's intentions. God doubts God's abilities. As writer Peter Rollins concludes from this earth-shattering scene: "To believe is human, to doubt, divine."[13]

If Jesus's own death and doubt reveal anything to us, it is that doubt *must* be a necessary part of life. Doubt is a gift, because it prevents us from being deceived into believing that anyone has gotten anything figured out. Doubt is a gift because it is the singular tool that can destroy our idols—our images of God, our arrogant claims to certainty—and help us fall into the true and living God, who is expansive and beyond the ability of our limited words to speak.

Job 11:7–9 says this brilliantly:

Can you fathom the mysteries of God? Can you probe the limits of the Almighty? They are higher than the heavens above—what can you do? They are deeper than the depths below—what can you know? Their measure is longer than the earth and wider than the sea.

True worship of this God, then, is not our declaration of certainty. It is not our confessions of creeds. It is not our assurance that all will be okay. No, true worship is to doubt. It is to embrace skepticism. It is recognizing our own propensity to want certainty and stability, and the realization that *those things are not possible*, but not only that, *they're not desirable*. We were not intended to know the answers to life's grand questions. We were intended, however, to walk with God. To bring our full, honest, true self to God. To open our eyes to perceive God, especially where we do not expect to find him. True faith is marked by persistent doubt. By persistent questioning. By persistent curiosity.

To be certain is to claim to have access to the mind of God. It is to have the hubris to assume that you could even fathom a molecule of accurate knowledge about God. But the good news is that everything you and I know is probably wrong. It probably falls short. Which means that we are invited on a journey of endless questioning. Of endless exploration. Of endlessly seeking for those rare but transformative moments where we do glimpse the glory of God. The response to doubt isn't to stop searching or speaking about ultimate things. No, it's the opposite. Again, Peter Rollins writes, "That which we cannot speak of is the one thing about whom and to whom we must never stop speaking."[14]

We cannot know God intellectually, but we can know God relationally. We cannot speak an accurate word about God, but we must never stop trying. Pope Francis says that "life is a journey, and when we stop, things don't go right."[15] If you want to lose a sense of purpose in life, then stop seeking. If you want to lose a sense of vitality, then stop trying to know God more. But if it is an abundant life you seek, a life of that is transfixed with the glory and beauty of reality, then you must keep exploring, wondering, and asking, because doubt is the very heart of faith.

16

Dry Bones

Have you ever found yourself in a state of utter despair, with nothing seeming right in your life or in your world, and every ounce of energy within you is gone? Have you ever experienced a collective feeling of hopelessness—perhaps an entire people, group, or nation that just feels tired, overwhelmed, and unable to envision a better future? We all walk through these seasons of life, and if you have not yet, you will.

Part of what makes life interesting, I believe, is the challenges we face and the various terrains that we trek through. Sometimes we have seasons of great abundance and satisfaction and sometimes we have seasons of pain, loss, and confusion. Both are necessary. Both have something to teach us. Both have the capability to refine and shape us into more mature, healthy individuals. But that truth doesn't make the bad seasons feel any less bad. It doesn't give us hope when the world around us is going up in flames. And if I am honest, I kind of feel like, as a nation, we're all in a state of hopelessness.

To listen to the discourse on every level of politics, from every party, today, is to quickly become discouraged that anything generative will ever get done at all. We talk past each other instead of to each other.

Beyond politics, I look around and see the major threats that face us all as humans—such as climate change, that threatens to end human civilization within a century if we do not change our course of action, and nationalism, which is nothing more than White supremacy and racism covered in frilly language. I look at the growing wealth disparities in our country and our world. I hear stories in every city of abuse, pain, and injustice. And I sometimes feel the flame of hope within my soul growing dim. When we're collectively entering into seasons of trials, seasons of despair, what are we to do? Is there a way for us to find hope, or at least to get some energy back to be able to do something productive with our lives to contribute to the healing of our world?

There is a passage from the book of Ezekiel in which I believe we can find some hope for our present moment. In Ezekiel chapter 37, it says,

> I felt the power of the Lord on me, and he brought me out by the Spirit of the Lord and put me down in the middle of a valley. It was full of bones. He led me around among the bones, and I saw that there were many bones in the valley and that they were very dry.
>
> Then he asked me, "Human, can these bones live?"
>
> I answered, "Lord God, only you know."
>
> He said to me, "Prophesy to these bones and say to them, 'Dry bones, hear the word of the Lord. This is what the Lord God says to the bones: I will cause breath to enter you so you will come to life. I will put muscles on you and flesh on you and cover you with skin. Then I will put breath in you so you will come to life. Then you will know that I am the Lord.'"
>
> So I prophesied as I was commanded. While I prophesied, there was a noise and a rattling. The bones came together, bone to bone. I looked and saw muscles come on the bones, and flesh grew, and skin covered the bones. But there was no breath in them.
>
> Then he said to me, "Prophesy to the wind. Prophesy, human, and say to the wind, 'This is what the Lord God

says: Wind, come from the four winds, and breathe on these
people who were killed so they can come back to life.'"

So I prophesied as the Lord commanded me. And the
breath came into them, and they came to life and stood
on their feet, a very large army.

Then he said to me, "Human, these bones are like all
the people of Israel. They say, 'Our bones are dried up,
and our hope has gone. We are destroyed.' So, prophesy
and say to them, 'This is what the Lord God says: My
people, I will open your graves and cause you to come
up out of your graves. Then I will bring you into the land
of Israel. My people, you will know that I am the Lord
when I open your graves and cause you to come up from
them. And I will put my Spirit inside you, and you will
come to life. Then I will put you in your own land. And
you will know that I, the Lord, have spoken and done it,
says the Lord.'"

We have a prophetic vision that God gives to the prophet
about the people of Israel. At the time that this prophecy came
to Ezekiel, the people of Israel were feeling collectively hopeless.
They were living in exile in Babylon, or modern-day Iraq, held
captive by the Babylonian Emperor named Nebuchadnezzar. This
king had not only enslaved the Jewish people, but he destroyed
their temple and ransacked Jerusalem.

In Judaism at this point, it was believed that God literally
dwelt in the temple. If the temple was allowed to be destroyed,
it could mean that God had left the people, separated from them
because of their injustice and sinful behavior. In this era of human
consciousness, almost everything was interpreted as an action of
God. If military victory or prosperity came, it was a sign of God's
blessing for right behavior. If there was destruction, famine, and
defeat, it was a sign of God's judgment for evil and wickedness.
When the temple is destroyed and the Jewish people begin to be
exiled in Iraq, they also begin to feel that God is judging them.

It's safe to say that the Jewish people felt pretty hopeless. They looked around the world, and the political unrest they saw looked like it would never end. They had, at this point, been a people continually in exile from their homeland. They faced famine, slavery, and oppression because of their faith in the God of Abraham. Any time they were brought back to their land and began to establish themselves, another empire would invade and destroy the progress they had accomplished. Nothing about their situation seemed hopeful. There was no possible vision for a better future.

This cycle of oppression and injustice is what they had gotten used to. It had been happening for centuries. So, they began to accept it. They began to accept the oppression as normal. They began to accept that this was their lot in life. Have you ever been there? So fatigued by the wrongdoing happening to you and around you that you eventually begin to accept it as normal? What once caused great anxiety and distress, now doesn't even cause you to bat an eyelash. I feel like this is exactly where we are at as a nation today.

We have accepted mass shootings as normal. They happen so often. We have accepted police violence on Black and Brown people as normal. It happens so often that we don't even hear about it. We've accepted childish, xenophobic rhetoric from thought leaders and public officials that it causes, at best, an eye roll when we hear it.

I also feel like this is where many of us are at in our lives. Every relationship seems to end in heartbreak and pain, so we just stop trying. We have no reason to believe it will ever work out for us. Our family continues to reject us because of who we are, so we've become numb to their rejection. The pain does not even well up within us anymore. Our health never seems to be getting better, so we give up and give in. We accept physical pain as part of our lives and stop seeking ways to be healthier.

Whatever it is—when we are overwhelmed by wrongdoing around us, as a natural defense and survival mechanism, we grow complacent. We stop feeling so deeply. We cut ourselves off. We begin to accept abnormalities as our reality. This is nothing to be ashamed of. It's a survival mechanism. But it is certainly not the abundant life that we were created to live. It's not the world that Jesus continually spoke about and prayed for. It is less than the life and the world we were designed to inhabit. This is where the people of Israel were at.

In this state of hopelessness. Many had given up on God—clearly, it seemed, God wasn't helping them. If he was, why did they continually find themselves in exile or oppressed? But it's in these moments that God often sends someone into our lives to speak a word that can change everything. It is in the moments when we're just about to give up hope that I have seen God do the most incredible miracles. The moments where we think we cannot go one step further, that's when deliverance shows up.

God gives a message to Ezekiel to share with the people in this most hopeless moment. And by the way, a prophet in the Bible is not a fortune teller. It is not someone who sees the future. In Scripture, a prophet is simply someone who surveys the landscape around them, looks at what's happening in the world, and speaks God's truth to it. If they see people walking in injustice and unrighteousness, they speak truth by calling them to repent, turn from their wicked ways, or prepare for the consequences of their behavior. They also can see visions of hope; they know that if the people follow God's moral code, if they walk uprightly, they will flourish.

In our day, we have prophets like this. People who are not afraid to speak the truth, to call out the powers that be, who shine a light on our collective sins and call us to change course or prepare for destruction. Prophets didn't end in the Hebrew Bible. God continues to raise up truth-tellers in our midst today. The question is, do we hear them? Are we willing to change our life? Change our way? To begin walking in a new path that may be more difficult but will lead us to wholeness and holiness? In this most hopeless moment, God sends Ezekiel. He sees a profound vision. Israel is in exile. Its people are in utter despair. They are a valley of dry bones.

In the Hebrew, the word *dry* here literally means downcast, depressed, hopeless. We see this same idea used in the Book of Proverbs 17:22 which says, "A cheerful heart is good medicine, but a crushed spirit dries up the bones." This vison is about the nation of Israel—they are "dry bones"—an army of dead, hopeless people. God shows Ezekiel this vision and then asks him, "O Mortal, do you think these bones can live?" This is a trick question. Ezekiel is looking out and seeing utter despair and death. These bones are decomposed, utterly lifeless. Obviously, in the normal course of things, these bones are never going to live again.

In the natural realm, they are about as dead as something can be. In the natural realm, there is no reason to have any hope that they can live again. But Ezekiel doesn't respond from the natural realm. He says, "Only you know, Oh Lord." He says, in my perspective, this situation looks pretty hopeless. But God, if you desire to bring life to this valley of death, you can do it. He trusts not in the circumstances in front of him. He trusts that what things appear to be right now don't guarantee the outcome.

Ezekiel is unwilling to just accept reality as it is. Ezekiel is willing to believe that change can happen. That this valley of dry, dead, hopeless bones may live again, if God wills it. So, he responds with faith, even when it seems pretty impossible to believe there could be a different future than what is in front of him. God then tells Ezekiel to speak to the bones, an act that in itself requires faith. How silly would this look? A man talking to dead, lifeless bones. A man speaking to something that cannot hear or respond to him.

Sometimes this is how faith works. We've got to move in faith, trusting in that which we cannot yet see, but we believe will come. You may not see a good partner for yourself, but if you walk in faith and act as if one is going to come, it's likely one will come. You may not see yourself getting healed from this disease, but if you walk in faith and believe and act like you're going to be healed, your chances of healing are exponentially increased. You may not think that your community will ever get out of its severe polarization, but unless you begin walking, talking, acting, and believing like it will, you will never see the potential for healing and transformation.

Ezekiel speaks to the bones, the words that God has told him to say: "I will cause breath to enter you so you will come to life. I will put muscles on you and flesh on you and cover you with skin. Then I will put breath in you so you will come to life. Then you will know that I am the Lord."

If these bones are hopeless people, just imagine how ridiculous Ezekiel must sound. The people have been in Babylonia for centuries. Their hope is just about gone, and Ezekiel says, "God is going to raise us up." We're going to have another chance. Deliverance is coming! The text continues:

> So I prophesied as I was commanded. While I prophesied, there was a noise and a rattling. The bones came together, bone to bone. I looked and saw muscles come on the bones, and flesh grew, and skin covered the bones. But there was no breath in them.

Before Ezekiel's eyes, the bones begin to become enfleshed again. In other words, Israel begins to see signs of hope. Signs of change. When the people take a step of faith and believe that a better tomorrow is possible, they begin to see real, tangible change. But also notice how that last verse ends: "But there was no breath in them." Wait a second.

The first line of God's promise through Ezekiel was, "I will cause breath to enter you so you will come to life," and yet, there was no breath in them. The bones were not yet alive. What good are bones covered in flesh if they are still dead? What good are minor signs of progress if they don't lead to substantive change? Isn't this how we think?

We are a people low on patience. We expect change to happen overnight. We expect the country to be healed in four years, once our candidate wins the White House. We expect the climate crisis to be remedied in a decade. We expect our own relationships to work out *right now*. We expect our career success to manifest *yesterday*. We lose hope and get discouraged, if success doesn't come quickly. Gradual signs of progress often go unnoticed. We give up too quickly when things don't happen in our time frame.

Ezekiel's prophecy took some time to come true. It was a process. The bones starting being put back together first; then flesh and muscle came upon them. Small signs of progress began to manifest in Israel. They weren't miraculously liberated overnight. A messiah did not just show up, destroy all the evil powers, and lead them into glory, and I bet, even as small changes began to manifest, many people got even less hopeful. It wasn't fast enough. Isn't that our human propensity?

We give up quickly. We miss the miracle because we reject the process. These dry bones are coming to life, but it's taking some time. The bodies are put together, but there is not yet breath in them. If they keep holding on, though, the breath will come. If you keep holding on, in faith, your liberation, your blessing, healing, and hope will return! Don't give up too soon. Don't lose hope too quickly!

Ezekiel calls upon the winds. The word wind in Hebrew is the word *ruach*, which also means breath and Spirit. So, there are layers of meaning here. Ezekiel is calling upon the Spirit of God, which is the source of life. He is also calling on the Spirit of the People of Israel to be revived. Their dry bones and downcast spirit are now being called to have life again.

As Ezekiel speaks, they rise. They believe. They have hope. They regain a sense of vision for a better tomorrow. In our own time, I really do believe God is speaking to some of us in the same way. Some of us who are feeling like giving up, or don't have the strength to go another week, or just don't want to give it another try. Some of us just can't imagine that things could get better.

If dead bones can rise, if Israel can be brought out of exile, you can step into a new life. You will make it past this rough season. You will see reconciliation and redemption. But you've got to rise up. You've got to choose to believe. You've got to prophesy, like Ezekiel, and speak to your dead circumstances and your discouragement. Speak truth where there are lies and words of light where darkness is thick. Whether it's hope for our nation, hope for our job, hope for your prognosis, hope for your relationships, know that change takes time. Know that progress doesn't happen suddenly most of the time.

This story reveals to us that our God is the resurrecting God. The God who can speak over a valley of dry bones and bring them new life. The God who can work in your life to heal your pain, to ignite the passion and fire that you've lost, to bring healing to your heart or body. This is the basis of our faith. That there is a God who cares for us and stands with us in our brokenness, waywardness, and pain. That this God desires to bring us into liberation, to free us from that which hinders us from joy and flourishing. That no matter how dry the valley of bones of our lives might be, that there is always hope of a new beginning and fresh start. And thanks be to God for that.

17

Holy Wars and Hypocrisy

Have you ever found yourself in an argument with someone, and then halfway through, like a lightning bolt, you have a moment of understanding, and you realize that this whole fight has been a huge adventure in missing the point? Or have you found yourself standing in opposition to a person or an issue—maybe political and maybe religious—and in the heat of it you're so certain you're right? However, when you step back and reflect on the situation, you realize that what had become a huge deal in the moment, was not actually a huge deal at all?

I find myself in situations like this often. Situations where I think I see, where I think I understand, where I think I am right. And then, when I step back and try to remove my emotions and my limited perspective and listen, I realize things are not always what they seem. We all do this, don't we? We divide against each other, form false boundaries, act from places of deep pain and hurt, and project that hurt on to one another and to entire groups of people?

We put up walls to separate us from the people we think we don't like. From the people we think are wrong. From the people we think are dangerous. But again, if we took a more objective look at a situation, if we tried to see from another's shoes, things might look very different.

Christians tend to be terrible at building bridges and proficient at erecting walls. We're known by others not for how we

reflect the loving way of Jesus but for how we often work hard to
do the exact opposite of what Jesus would do. This isn't just one
cynical Christian's perspective—it's well documented across our
culture. We all have heard the quote often attributed to Mahatma
Gandhi, which searingly declares, "I like your Christ. I do not like
your Christians. Your Christians are so unlike your Christ."

One of the areas that Christian hypocrisy can be seen most
clearly is when we talk about sex and sexual ethics. Christian
churches have created all sorts of rules and regulations to police
people's sex lives and sexuality, to make people conform or feel
ashamed if they don't line up with our sexual ethics, but then
we declare that war is holy and churches support our government in dividing and battling our "enemies." Yet the truth is that
in Scripture, nothing could be less clear than what God desires
for humans sexually. Despite what's been preached over and over
again, there is a lot of ambiguity in the Bible's teaching about sex,
especially when you move beyond modern English translations
and return to the original Greek and Hebrew texts of Scripture.
The sexual ethics of the Bible are messy, inconsistent, and often,
really disturbing.

But the Bible is abundantly clear on many topics that are
treated as hopelessly complex by the church such as violence
and war. Jesus says, "Love your enemies." "Bless those who curse
you." "Turn the other cheek." "Do not return evil for evil." That
is about as black and white as one can get—no interpretation is
needed here. Nonviolence is the unambiguous message of Jesus.

We have created false rules and boundaries, hypocritical standards based on misunderstandings of the Bible. And we use them
to hurt and divide from others. In her song "Holy War," Alicia
Keys calls out the hypocrisy of the Christian church, saying that
we've been "Baptized in boundaries, schooled in sin"—suggesting
that the church has declared "holy" a set of unethical boundaries
and false rules, and that the church has schooled us in sin. In other
words, she suggests that we have declared holy that which God
says is not holy. These false boundaries divide us; they cause us

to fear one another based on artificial differences that don't matter: our ethnic differences, our theological differences, our sexual differences. These are the bricks in the false walls we build that divide us. That keep us from understanding one another, locking us in boxes of prejudice and misunderstanding.

How many of us know that it is true that when we hold on to grudges and misunderstandings, we're the ones tormented inside? How sad is it when we judge, push away, and condemn others based on a misunderstanding or our own limited perspective and refusal to humble ourselves and try to see the humanity in the face of another.

This problem is not new. It is not unique to our day and age. In the Bible, we read account after account of folks judging, condemning, and hurting each other based on artificial differences. God speaks some powerful wisdom to us in these circumstances.

Much like churches today, the early church was divided by racial predudice. Even the earliest leaders—I am thinking now of the Apostle Peter—struggled with racial bias against Gentiles (non-Jews). He resisted God's call to share the Gospel with them. He didn't want them to be included in this new Jesus movement. This attitude spread throughout many of the earliest Christian communities. There was a great deal of judgment and fear leveled at people who were of different ethnicity or cultural background. The Greek churches divided against the Jewish churches. The Jewish churches divided against the Greek churches. But the Apostle Paul had been convicted by God to rid them all of these artificial boundaries of race. So, he wrote a letter to a local church in the Greek city of Ephesus, and confronted this division head on:

> Therefore, remember that formerly you who are Gentiles by birth and called "uncircumcised" by those who call themselves "the circumcised" (which is done in the body by human hands)—remember that at that time you were separate from Christ, excluded from citizenship in Israel and foreigners to the covenants of the promise, without

hope and without God in the world. But now in Christ
Jesus you who once were far away have been brought
near by the blood of Christ. (Ephesians 2:11–13, NIV)

Paul is talking to Gentiles who are dividing themselves against
Jewish believers. He reminds them that at one time, during the Old
Covenant, they were in fact excluded from citizenship in Israel,
which by the way is not the "nation" of Israel, but when it's used
in the New Testament, it literally means the Kingdom of God, or
God's community of grace. He says that it is true that at one point
they had postured themselves against God and against God's people.

And then he says, you were once excluded from God's Kingdom, but in Jesus Christ you have now been included. That is
good news. And how did Jesus bring these people, who were once
far away, into the Kingdom of God? Paul continues:

For he himself is our peace, who has made the two
groups one and has destroyed the barrier, the dividing
wall of hostility, by setting aside in his flesh the law with
its commands and regulations. His purpose was to create
in himself one new humanity out of the two, thus making
peace, and in one body to reconcile both of them to God
through the cross, by which he put to death their hostility.
He came and preached peace to you who were far away
and peace to those who were near. For through him we
both have access to the Father by one Spirit. (Ephesians
2:13–18, NIV)

He says that Jesus came and showed us a better way. A way
that destroys our barriers. A way that moves us beyond artificial
rules and standards. He says Jesus made two groups one by setting aside the law with its commands and regulations.

Jesus was a faithful Jewish believer during his life, but he
also had little tolerance for the way that religious rules and standards were used to exclude, control, and judge other people. Jesus

believed that to be faithful to God meant being loving toward others, more than following rules. Jesus continually frustrated the religious leaders of his day because of this—he disregarded boundaries to be compassionate toward everyone. This is what Paul means when he says that Jesus "set aside the law and its commands." And if Jesus set aside these things, favoring love and grace, then what laws and commands, what arbitrary rules are we using to judge others? To divide from others?

Are there people in your life that you judge and separate from because they embrace different political views than you? Are there people you judge and separate from because they embrace different theological beliefs about God or the Bible? Are there people whom you judge and separate from because they embrace different ethics in regard to dating or sex? Do you judge and separate from others because they embrace a different understanding of how certain things should be done in your workplace, or at home, or in your church?

I believe that we all have people that we have allowed misunderstandings and false boundaries to keep us from. False rules and expectations hold us back from extending this person or people the dignity and respect they deserve, and every time we place another brick in our wall of judgment and separation toward others, the more boxed in we're becoming. The more we're preventing ourselves from growing, healing, and expanding. Your judgment of others isn't only damaging to them, it is damaging you, and this flies in the face of the example and teaching of Jesus our Lord. Why? Paul says,

> His purpose was to create in himself one new humanity out of the two, thus making peace, and in one body to reconcile both of them to God through the cross, by which he put to death their hostility. He came and preached peace to you who were far away and peace to those who were near. For through him we both have access to the Father by one Spirit. (Ephesians 2:14–15, NIV)

Jesus was crucified specifically because he offended everyone by disregarding their rules and boundaries. He offended the Gentiles by calling out their government and their colonizing systems as unjust and against God's will. He offended Jewish people by disregarding certain laws of the Hebrew Bible that caused them to separate from Gentiles who also wanted to experience God's embracing grace and love. Ultimately, his behavior caused both groups to respond with hatred, with a desire to kill him, because sometimes when we mess with "sacred boundaries" people get really angry.

Sometimes when we are called to repent of our racism, sexism, homophobia, false idols, our desire for the "way things have always been," we feel like we need to defend or attack. We launch holy wars. We tell ourselves that we are in the right. We refuse to see the perspective of another. We refuse to rethink where we're standing and how we're thinking. This caused the powers that be to attack and kill Jesus.

The Scriptures tell us that Jesus did so willingly, in order for us who call him Lord to be able to look up at his example on the cross and see where our false boundaries and walls end—in crucifixion and in death. Death of relationships. Death of our values. Death of communities. Death of countries. Nothing can bring pain and destruction to your friendships more than erecting false borders, making people hold to standards that are not fair, or are not right. Nothing can bring pain and destruction to a community than fighting to uphold our prejudices, biases, and judgments above the call to love and seek the good of one another.

Instead, Paul tells us that Christ sought to make one new humanity. Isn't that an incredible statement? In the church at Ephesus the Greeks and Jews were separating. Paul says that Christ desires to create one new humanity in which those arbitrary aspects of our identity are no longer used to separate us, but rather are celebrated as we come together. We are better when we are in community with people who see the world differently. We are better when we are made a bit uncomfortable by allowing someone to do something differently than we are used to.

God's plan is to call us into relationship across differences and divides, to be one people who do life with one another. As we seek to be at peace with all people and as we seek to be in relationship with people who see the world differently, we're challenged to grow and expand. Dividing is easy. It is easy to silo ourselves in our echo chamber where everyone thinks and looks and acts like us. But when we choose the path of building walls, or launching attacks at each other from a distance, we only bring more pain to ourselves. That is when our lives begin to wither on the vine. That's when our relationships become toxic. That's when we cease to grow. That's where sin flourishes.

Paul reminds us:

> He came and preached peace to you who were far away and peace to those who were near. For through him we both have access to the Father by one Spirit. (Ephesians 2:17, NIV)

Christ's desire is to bring peace where there is division. To reveal that despite our surface-level disagreements, we are and have always been participating in *one common Spirit*. What would our world look like if we believed that and acted accordingly? If we put the dignity of each other ahead of being right or agreeing on every ethical or theological idea? What if our response to those who offend us or wrong us was *radical forgiveness* as Jesus taught?

Again, this is far easier said than done. When somebody hurts me, it's my natural inclination to want to retaliate. I want to demand that they apologize and make it right. The problem with this line of thinking is that I give the one who hurt me the ultimate power over my healing. What if they never choose to apologize? What if they never make things right? Then my wound festers. Then my anger and pain fester, and my soul becomes infected.

But what if we do as Jesus taught—fight through our pain to extend forgiveness? That can seem like injustice to us, can't it? But there is deeper wisdom in Jesus's teaching. If we do wrong to those who wrong us, no one wins. We both have committed a wrong. We both bear the guilt and shame that comes from doing wrong, and we perpetuate the cycle of wrongdoing. But when we forgive those who wrong us and refuse to retaliate, we short-circuit the cycle of violence.

This is what Jesus embodied up to the last moments of his life. On the cross, as he's being mocked and murdered, he looks at his tormentors' eyes and declares, "Father forgive them." Those words. That grace. I can only imagine it broke the hearts of those who listened. How could he forgive them after all that they had done to him? Yet he shows that only forgiveness has the power to break the cycle of violence. It holds a mirror to the person who has done wrong and forces them to look at their wrong and confront it. It frees the offended party from being stuck in anger, waiting for others to change or seek reconciliation.

Extending forgiveness liberates us. It is perhaps one of the most radical acts we can do. It's what is so desperately needed in our world. How would your life change if you worked to forgive that abusive parent? How would your life change if you extended grace and love to that person who did you wrong? What message would that send to them? What would that do to your heart and life? This is a hard path, but it's the holy one. It's the path that leads us to the life and the world that God desires for us.

But the hard truth that far too many of us know is this: when we've been hurt by others, when we bear our own wounds, it is really hard to want to forgive. In fact, in our wounding, we often want nothing more than to build a wall to protect ourselves from further hurt, and there is a time and space for that to be sure. But we cannot stay behind the walls that we build. The wisdom of Jesus calls us to another way: to forgive. What if, right now, you took a deep breath and sent loving and forgiving energy to the person who has done you wrong? What if, right now, you surrendered the pain and the wounding to God? What if, right now, you chose to try to see your circumstances and situation from the perspective of another?

Maybe you'd be free. Maybe healing would begin. Maybe the dividing walls would begin to crumble. Maybe we would begin to see the one new humanity that Jesus is seeking to create in our world. Paul concludes this portion of his letter saying these words:

> Consequently, you are no longer foreigners and strangers, but fellow citizens with God's people and also members of his household, built on the foundation of the apostles and prophets, with Christ Jesus himself as the chief cornerstone. (Ephesians 2:19–22, NIV)

He is declaring a spiritual truth. He is saying that in the spiritual realm, there are no foreigners or strangers, there is no in group and out group, there is no us versus them. In the spiritual realm, we're all citizens of God's Kingdom and members of God's household. The call is for us to make this spiritual reality real in our physical lives and world. The call is to seek reconciliation with all our heart. The call is to repent of our false barriers and prejudices and seek to see the world through the eyes of God's Spirit.

For when God looks at your life, he doesn't see enemies and friends. He doesn't see the right and the wrong. He sees one new humanity. He says one world filled with his children. A world where people make mistakes and mess up. But a world where, through the power of grace, healing and restoration are possible. May this become our truth and reality. May we end our endless holy wars through the power of reckless, messy, counter-intuitive grace.

18

Truth Doesn't Need Defending

What are we talking about when we talk about truth? On one hand, the answer seems pretty obvious. On the other hand, especially in our current age, understanding exactly what we mean when we say "truth" is pretty elusive. After all, we live in the era of "fake news." The era when those who have the most power and privilege are often the most dishonest and untruthful. And we live in the shadow of an era of postmodernity when all concepts of truth have been thoroughly deconstructed, and something new seems to be emerging in their place.

In my own journey, the churches that spoke the most about so-called truth were also those who used that truth to beat me into conformity to their idea of what it was to be a man, to be a Christian, and to be a person. I grew up in an independent, fundamentalist, Bible-believing, Baptist church—those were the literal words on our church's sign out front. In that context, truth was absolutely the highest value.

Faith was not about leaping into the darkness or stepping beyond a boundary with confidence that someone or something would be there to catch us, but about being certain of that which could not readily be seen or experienced, and out of that certainty, to combat any idea that didn't align with our construction of the truth.

Honestly, it was really nice to be in a place where, at twelve years old, I had all of the truth figured out. I had all of the answers to all of life's questions and challenges. Or so I was told.

The truth in my world was purely propositional—it was the right answers to the hard questions. It was cognitive and reasonable. Anyone could have the truth if they just believed in it and memorized it—or bought the book. But as I got older, and as our world became more globalized and more interconnected through the explosion of the internet and social media, many, if not most, of the so-called truths I received began to be called into question. My lived reality didn't seem to align with what I was told to be objectively and eternally true. And my understanding of God, who honestly had become nothing more than some grand, human in the sky who dictated all of those truths and expected us all to get A-pluses on our truth exam, lest we be damned to the Lake of Fire, began to fall apart because of my experience of God moving in places that the truth said God couldn't be or among people who flatly rejected the truth.

I also began to experience a great deal of fear from the people that I looked up to and learned the truth from because I began asking questions, reading books, and hanging with people who they thought had abandoned the truth. When I saw that fear, I began to be very concerned: why would someone who had the absolutely and eternal truth be afraid of people asking questions or posing challenges? Truth should have nothing to be afraid of. At the end of the day, after all of the challenges and critiques, the truth, if it is indeed true, should remain standing unscathed, right? After coming from an environment of truth like this, I began to resent anyone who talked about truth in an objective way. Truth, in my experience, was just a battering ram created by those in power to marginalize, oppress, and beat people into conformity. Why would I want anything to do with that?

I spent a good number of years spiraling into the wild world of extreme postmodernism and existentialism, where I basically said that the truth was either nonexistent or unattainable, so screw it all, let's eat, drink, and be merry, for tomorrow we die. Anyone else been there? But living in a world without a sense of truth or grounding also became a bit of a hellish existence for me. Because somewhere, deep within, I just know that there is something called truth.

There is some ground of being on which my life and all of reality sits upon. There is some logic, reason, or intelligence in the universe that seems to in some mysterious way be guiding or creating or experimenting or directing the affairs of the cosmos. And that force or being or intelligence seems to have established laws or principles that govern the affairs of our universe. In other words, out of my extreme deconstruction and distaste for the truth as I experienced it, I began to discover that, for me, living in the nihilistic, deconstructed, absurdist world where I believed there was no truth was not right or sustainable either. Instead, what emerged out of my deconstruction was that there is something called truth, but what we talk about truth is actually the same thing we talk about when we talk about God.

On June 2, 2016, NASA released a press release that read: "Hubble Finds That the Universe Is Expanding Faster Than Expected." It opened with the following statement:

> Astronomers using NASA's Hubble Space Telescope have discovered that the universe is expanding 5 percent to 9 percent faster than expected. "This surprising finding may be an important clue to understanding those mysterious parts of the universe that make up 95 percent of everything and don't emit light, such as dark energy, dark matter and dark radiation," said study leader and Nobel Laureate Adam Riess of the Space Telescope Science Institute and Johns Hopkins University, both in Baltimore, Maryland.

There are two things I want to point out from this press release. First of all, NASA says that 95 percent of everything in the universe is mysterious.

Humans have only begun to grasp and understand maybe 5 percent of our universe, what it is, what composes it, how it works. I point this out to say that no matter what I say here, no matter what anyone says ever, we must proceed through our lives with humility. The smartest astrophysicists and astronomers don't know even 5 percent about how reality works, so it's pretty safe to say that most of us have very little understanding of anything. So, when we talk about truth, we need to talk and walk with humility.

Secondly, we live in a universe that is expanding. For many of us, that is not news. But for some, it may be. Reality is not set in stone. It is not static. It's always expanding, changing, growing. Our universe and reality itself have not ceased the process of creation. It's ongoing. If this is true, and we believe in a concept of God, then it is also safe to rationally deduce that our God must be *at least* as big as the universe at this moment and, likely, must be bigger than the universe itself.

It can also be suggested that perhaps Godself is expanding along with the universe that God created. As French theologian and scientist Teilhard de Chardin posited, "Christ has a cosmic body that extends throughout the universe."[16] At the core of the Christian conception of the Divine has always been an understanding that the very light and life that creates the universe is God, and that God is incarnated in all of reality. This is what the New Testament speaks of time and time again when it says, speaking of the Cosmic Christ:

> For by him were all things created, that are in heaven, and that are in earth, visible and invisible, whether they be thrones, or dominions, or principalities, or powers: all things were created by him, and for him: And he is before all things, and in him all things find their being. (Colossians 1:16, NIV)

My point in saying all of this is that the universe we exist in is always expanding. Therefore, it is a logical assumption that

God is at least as expansive as the universe, and may, in fact, be expanding with it. And if my earlier statement that God and truth are synonymous, then we can say that truth is really, really big and always getting bigger.

The ancients talked about the bigness and mysteriousness of God and the universe in terms of time: they used a word in Greek *aiónios*, to talk about how big God is. In our Bible, it is translated as eternal, unending, in other words, a really, really long time. The ancients juxtapose this talk by speaking of humans in relation to our smallness and finitude. In fact, one of the most bad-ass sections in Scripture is when God speaks to Job about God's bigness and Job's smallness:

> Where were you when I laid the foundations of the earth? Tell me, if you know so much.

> Who determined its dimensions and stretched out the surveying line?

> What supports its foundations, and who laid its cornerstone as the morning stars sang together and all the angels shouted for joy? (Job 30:4–11, ESV)

And he goes on for four chapters saying the same kind of things. Basically, God is looking at Job, and in fact, all of humanity, and saying, "Calm yourselves down. You don't know *anything*." Again, great humility is required when we are talking about truth.

When we begin to conceive of the bigness of God, of the universe, and of reality, it becomes really clear very quickly that we can't know very much. God is infinite and we are finite. The truth is far bigger than our minds, bodies, or souls could ever grasp. In more philosophical terms, we would say that God is objective and we are subjective. That simply means that we are subjects or must bow to the object that is reality. We cannot grasp God, but God can grasp us.

The same can be said for truth. There is absolutely something called truth. There are principles and ideas and laws and realities that exist in the universe, and we may be able to comprehend and understand and use some of those realities to our benefit and to our own personal growth and evolution. But we will never be able to grasp it. We will always be subject to the truth. Our finite minds will always bow before truth in humility and awe, because it is the thing that all of us desire most, but it is also the one thing that none of us can ever fully grasp.

One of the last things that Jesus teaches his disciples before the end of his life is that they should continue to listen and be attuned to the Spirit of God, who will "guide [humanity] into all truth" (John 16:13). The idea, here, is that all of the truth has not been revealed or explored, and that the Spirit will continue to lead humans into deeper and broader and wider understanding. We have a trajectory from the beginning of the Scriptures to the end of Scriptures that outlines the trajectory of human evolution.

Starting with the myth of Genesis, we begin in darkness, and then light begins to expand. We begin with a God who is initially afraid of humans pursuing knowledge and grasping for truth, and we end with one who is called the incarnation of God showing us that truth is dynamic, not static, and that we should continue to seek it out through the expansion of our minds. If, in Christian consciousness, truth and God are synonymous, then Christians necessarily believe that in the person of Jesus, truth became flesh. And as truth became flesh in Jesus, we also learn from another angle that truth is not static. It is dynamic and relational. It grows and progresses and evolves and is different based on context.

The call of Christ is the call to continued exploration, to continued curiosity, and to continued questioning. And the more that we lean into the pursuit of truth, we will also be led into a posture of what could be called worship, or holy reverence and awe at the bigness and beauty and mysteriousness of the cosmos. This, I believe, is what the life of faith is ultimately all about.

When we adopt truth as Jesus embodied it—as poignant, powerful, and yet ever expanding—then we must be willing to speak up boldly for what we believe is right, good, and true, while nonetheless holding a posture of humility, willing to repent or expand our perspectives as we experience truth through other perspectives. This is the tension of truth that each of us is called to live into.

Every day, we are called to live in awe and curiosity of absolute truth. We are called to observe and note the factual truth. And both of these create the context where we create a by-product called our truth, or the truth as we've understood it and believe it today. If we are to live whole lives, we must always seek to live in alignment with the truth as we experience and understand it, knowing that it will expand, progress, and change over time.

Over the course of our lives, our perspectives change. But at every stage of our lives, we also are only capable of living according to the truth as we understand it. Whenever we try to live out of sync with *our truth*, our lives tend to go awry. For instance, when we find ourselves in a community of faith that we no longer align with, if we try to stick around in that community for long enough, we will find our stress levels increasing, our happiness and health decreasing, and our sense of peace and joy destroyed. Marginalized people know about this in a profoundly real way; if you are made to feel inferior, or forced to try to hide your true self from the world around you, you will find the pressure within bottling up, and your life will suffer from this lack of authenticity.

To live according to our truth is a dangerous and beautiful task, and it is absolutely necessary to live a meaningful life. To embrace the world as we see it, and live according to reality as we perceive it, is dangerous because it brings us into conflict with others who see the world very differently. This is why grace is so necessary. When we live with a posture of awe and curiosity, mixed with our conviction, we begin to see other perspectives as just that: *different understandings of the very thing we're all grasping for.* That means we can disagree boldly, and say, "I think that's wrong," but we have no reason to be defensive. Because remember, truth doesn't need to be defended. It needs to be incarnated.

If there is any core message that Christianity uniquely offers the world, it is this. That truth is relational, dynamic, and incarnated. Life is truth. Living is truth. And anytime we divorce our conception of truth from our incarnated reality, we create a dangerous division that ultimately only causes destruction. Truth divorced from incarnated reality becomes a battering ram for the privileged and powerful to beat people into conformity. Truth that is incarnated is held with conviction, curiosity, and humility. We can say, "This is how I see things from where I stand, but I am willing to listen and observe others with curiosity. Even so, I will speak and live from the truth as I understand it now."

If we get into this rhythm and posture of exploration, humility, and authenticity, and become people who live our truths, I believe our lives, families, and communities will be better for it. When we speak truth boldly and with passion, I believe we'll begin to see society transformed into the more just and equal world. When we live as humble and curious subjects to the great object of the universe, we'll find beauty pulsating through every moment of every day. In this way, Jesus was absolutely right when he said: "Know the truth, and it will make you free" (John 8:32).

19

A Light in Our Darkness

In the beginning was the Word, and the Word was with God, and the Word was God. He was in the beginning with God. All things came into being through him, and without him not one thing came into being. What has come into being in him was life, and the life was the light of all people. The light shines in the darkness, and the darkness did not overcome it.

There was a man sent from God, whose name was John. He came as a witness to testify to the light, so that all might believe through him. He himself was not the light, but he came to testify to the light. The true light, which enlightens everyone, was coming into the world. (John 1:1–9)

These are words from the first chapter of the Gospel named for John. They echo words written by the Prophet Isaiah 1, five hundred years earlier: "The people who walk in darkness will see a great light. For those who live in a land of deep darkness, a light will shine" (Isaiah 9:2). Throughout the Bible there is a consistent story about light expelling darkness. Genesis says that there was nothing but darkness until God spoke, declaring "Let there be light!" and as light dawned for the first time on the canvas of creation, life itself was born.

From that first light, vegetation began to spring from the ground, waters began to flow, animals of all types appeared on the surface of the planet, and human beings emerged, bearing the image of the Creator, relying on the light of the sun as the source of life.

It can be argued that light is the most important force in all of creation. Without it, we cannot see or be seen. We cannot grow or live. Light reveals the truth about reality. Light both warms our bodies and shows us the way that we are supposed to go. The Scriptures declare that God *is* light, and the light is life itself. Therefore, anyone who has life, has God. And anyone who has God, has the light. This is why Jesus said, "You are the Light of the world" (Matthew 5:14)! He taught us that we had the power to bring life, to be life, and to shine gloriously. But also, from the earliest pages of Scripture, we learn that while humans are fundamentally partakers in the light of God, we often stumble into deep darkness. We lose our way. We act outside of our nature. We begin to bring destruction, injustice, and suffering to all that's around us.

Our light is buried beneath layers of deceit and greed. And as the light dims, we grow colder, more disoriented. Our life is drained of us. We move further from our truest identity as children of the light, and live in a state of confusion about who we are and what the world is about. In it is the metaphor of darkness that we wander far from home. We become sojourners and nomads, lost in the desert, longing for someone to point out the way back home.

It is in a period of darkness and confusion that Jesus was born two thousand years ago. It was a day in which the Hebrew people were living under the oppressive rule of the Roman Empire, under the reign of Caesar Augustus, an emperor who loved his power, privilege, and wealth, and lived to protect it at their expense. Herod the Great was the governor of Jerusalem, and he was coming to the end of a long, bloody career. He ruled through tactics of terror.

The Jewish people were also greatly divided among themselves, fighting over minute religious and doctrinal issues. There were four competing sects in Second Temple Judaism of the first century, and these led to constant friction, only increased by the oppressive rule of Rome. Riots were common. Tension was unceasing. There was no unified Jewish identity, and people were growing increasingly hopeless. The first-century Palestinian world was one that was growing increasingly dark. It was a world filled with crises on the brink of chaos. A world not unlike our own.

It is into this world that the stories of the Gospel tell us that Jesus emerged. Into this darkness, the light and love of Christ first burst forth. In the midst of this division, Christ reveals a path for reconciliation through his example of self-sacrificial love. In the midst of this oppression, Christ reveals the path for liberation through the overturning of oppressive systems and the establishment of communities where everyone is given what they need and everyone is equal. In the face of violent, tyrannical, egocentric, hedonistic rulers, Jesus emerges as a Prince of Peace, and declares that the Kingdom of God is ruled by the least of us, the poor, the marginalized, and powerless. Into a cold, dark, bleak reality, the warmth and light of Christ emerges as a signpost of hope and redemption.

It is this light, this hope that we focus on each year at Christmastime. It is the joy that comes from the sudden realization that all is not lost, that there is a better way, that God has not forsaken us, and that our liberation draws near that we sing about around our Christmas trees. The message and meaning of Christmas are simply that when the world seems most overwhelmingly dim, the light of the world will do whatever it needs to break through the dark and dense shell, and reveal to us a reason for hope and a path to redemption.

The Christmas story that we've heard told tells of just how great a length our God has gone to bring us redemption. The King of Glory would humble himself, taking on flesh, and entering into the world as a helpless baby, born out of wedlock to a young, poor, peasant girl. At his birth, there was no midwife, no crib, and no warm blankets. Instead, God chose to enter the world in the same way that the most oppressed people did—born among the dust and dirt, among common farm animals, wrapped in leftover scraps of cloths.

In this image, we realize that God is not like the tyrannical kings who ruled the world, seeking power and glory for themselves, but instead God locks arms in solidarity with those who have been cast down, thrown out, and who are seen as burdens and blights on the rest of society. In this image, we also find the simple yet radical message of how we can find personal redemption: through humbling ourselves, disconnecting from material possessions and pursuits of worldly power, and through giving generously, loving wildly, and finding joy and gratitude in each moment. In that baby in Bethlehem, we see an image and icon of what it means to live in the light. We see revealed what truly makes life worth living. All that is important is there around the bed: family, peace, joy, and love in the simplicity of life. From that manger, a beam of light radiates through the darkness, extending an invitation to us all to return to what matters most.

Isn't it true that when someone is filled with light and life, we feel drawn to them? No matter how big or small, no matter how seemingly important a person is who is filled with light, we gravitate to them because they seem to have something that we are deeply longing for: satisfaction and joy. Even when light shines through this little baby boy, astrologers from the east are drawn to him. Shepherds leave their sheep in the fields and flock to his bedside. The angels surround him, singing songs of joy. In the midst of the darkness, light has dawned and hope has come. A path to redemption from the darkness has burst forth on the scene, and everyone is captivated.

I believe that the story of the birth of Christ is more important and meaningful than ever. We stand at a fork in the road. Will we take the path of light or the path of darkness? Will we cling tightly to our power and privilege, or will we willingly give it up for the good of others? This is the question that Christmas calls us to contemplate now, and this is the message that Christ calls us to contemplate every day. We have a great reason to hope and to sing. God has come to us in the person of Jesus, and stands among the poor, the marginalized, the cast out, broken down, and beaten up. God has taken the side of the underdog, and has declared that a day of justice and equity will one day come in its fullness.

Christmas is a celebration of what God has brought to us in Jesus, and a precelebration for the day that God has promised to bring about in the future, when all people follow in the example of Jesus, and love boldly, walk with humility, and give generously. A day when all that is broken in this world is healed and all of the systems of oppression are flattened. One of my favorite lines from Handel's "The Hallelujah Chorus" is toward the end of the song where Handel quotes the Book of Revelation and proclaims:

> The Kingdom of this world, it has become, the Kingdom of our Lord and of his Christ, and he shall reign for ever and ever. (Revelation 11:15)

That's what we celebrate at Christmastime, and that's why I still love Christmas. There's a new kind of king with a new kind of kingdom. In the third and fourth verses of "Joy to the World," Isaac Watts penned these words:

> No more let sin or sorrows grow, nor thorns infest the ground. He comes to make his blessings flow far as the curse is found. He rules the world with truth and grace, and makes the nations prove the glories of his righteous-ness, and wonders of his love.

This joy is linked to the new day that God is bringing about, when the curses of darkness, of suffering, of injustice are over-turned by the blessing of God—when the one righteous ruler, the God who is love, rules over us all with truth, grace, and love. This is what those shepherds and wise men saw in the person of Jesus some two thousand years ago. This is what Jesus embodied and taught as he lived his life. And this is the heartbeat and hope of the Gospel.

God is with us. God loves us so much that he desires to be with us, even in the midst of our brokenness and suffering. And more than that, God desires to bless us, to make all that is wrong in our lives and in our world right. God desires to redeem us. To shine light into the depths of our lives and expel the darkness.

Acknowledgments

This book was birthed during some of the most transformative and difficult years of my life personally, and I believe of our society collectively. I am so grateful for the people who walked alongside me through these turbulent years as colleagues and friends in ministry, navigating uncharted territories together in our San Diego clergy group: Rev. Wendy Holland, Rev. Matthew Hambrick, Rev. Colin Matthewson, Rev. Laurel Matthewson, and Rev. Matthew Nault.

I am also very grateful to the congregations I have been blessed to serve in this season: Missiongathering Christian church and Metanoia church. These progressive, inclusive communities truly embody what it means to embrace the path of Jesus and have helped me become a more faithful disciple—so thank you.

I am especially grateful to my agent Cathleen Falsani and my editor Jon Sweeney for having a vision for this book and working with me to bring it to life.

I've always believed that God is most powerfully experienced in and through those who surround us, and I've certainly experienced the love and grace of God through you all. So, *thank you.*

NOTES

[1] Nathan Lopes Cardozo, "Purim and Its Irrelevance," *David Cardozo Academy*, October 7, 2015, www.cardozoacademy.org/thoughtstoponder/purim-and-its-irrelevance2/.

[2] Martin Luther King, Jr., "Out of the Long Night of Segregation," *Missions: An International Baptist Magazine*, February 8, 1958.

[3] Osho, "Spiritually Serious Emerson?," Ch. 7 "Freedom Is the Ultimate Value," Osho Online Library, 2004, www.osho.com/osho-online-library/osho-talks/spirituality-seriousness-emerson-a56efba0-450?p=49a9096b2df0abc64ea45b0357f01404.

[4] William O'Brien, "Jesus the Racist," *Geez Magazine*, September 22, 2012, geezmagazine.org/magazine/article/jesus-the-racist.

[5] Barry Corey, "The Radical Call of Kindness," *Biola Magazine,* Biola University, June 1, 2016, www.biola.edu/blogs/biola-magazine/2016/the-radical-call-of-kindness.

[6] Maggie Haberman, "Inside Trump Tower, an Increasingly Upset and Alone Donald Trump," *New York Times*, October 9, 2016, www.nytimes.com/2016/10/10/us/politics/trump-tower.html.

[7] Teresa of Avila, *The Complete Works of St. Teresa of Jesus* (Kansas City, MO: Sheed & Ward, 1982), 327.

[8] Thomas Merton, *New Seeds of Contemplation* (New York: New Directions, 1972), 226–28.

[9] Henri J. M. Nouwen, *Life of the Beloved: Spiritual Living in a Secular World* (New York: Crossroad, 2002), 106.

[10] Bessel A. van der Kolk, *The Body Keeps the Score: Brain, Mind, and Body in the Healing of Trauma* (New York: Penguin Books, 2015), 235.

[11] Quoted in Elliott S. Horowitz, *Reckless Rites: Purim and the Legacy of Jewish Violence* (Princeton, NJ: Princeton University Press, 2008).

[12] "Infancy Gospel of James," trans. M. R. James, *Infancy Gospel of Thomas, Greek Text A,* www.earlychristianwritings.com/text/infancythomas-a-mrjames.html.

[13] Peter Rollins, *Insurrection: To Believe Is Human, to Doubt, Divine* (New York: Howard Books, 2011).

[14] Peter Rollins, *How (Not) to Speak of God* (Brewster, MA: Paraclete Press, 2011), xvi.

[15] Pope Francis, "Pope Francis Quotes," *Jesuit Resource*, Xavier University, 2016, www.xavier.edu/jesuitresource/online-resources/quote-archive1/pope-francis.

[16] Pierre Teilhard de Chardin, "Cosmic Life," *The Library of Teilhard de Chardin*, www.organism.earth/library/document/cosmic-life.

About the Author

Brandan Robertson is a noted author, progressive Christian minister, activist, and public theologian working at the intersections of spirituality, sexuality, and social renewal.

He is the author of eight books on spirituality, justice, and theology, including the INDIES Book of the Year Award Finalist, *True Inclusion: Creating Communities of Radical Embrace,* and the Amazon best-selling devotional *Strength in Faith.* Robertson has bylines in *TIME Magazine, San Diego Union Tribune, the Huffington Post, NBC,* and the *Washington Post.* As a trusted voice on progressive faith and politics, he is regularly interviewed in national and global media outlets including *National Public Radio,* the *Independent UK,* the *New York Times,* and *POLITICO.* In July 2021, *Rolling Stone* included Robertson in its annual "Hot List" of top artists, creatives, and influencers who *"are giving us reason to be excited about the future."* He received his Bachelor of Arts in Pastoral Ministry and Theology from Moody Bible Institute, his Master of Theological Studies from Iliff School of Theology, and a Master of Arts in Political Science and Public Administration from Eastern Illinois University. He currently resides in Washington, DC.